WELCOME

From the dispute over who made the first landing to the end of the Cold War, aircraft carrier aviation changed beyond all recognition.

Nobody can quite agree on who first landed a jet on an aircraft carrier. Was it the legendary test pilot taking part in a complex development programme, or the anonymous junior officer taking a desperate gamble that paid off? Either way, by the end of 1945, it was clear that the future of aircraft carriers lay with jet propulsion.

And despite many predictions of the carrier's demise, that future turned out to be rich and incident-packed. Far from dwindling away, the carrier went from strength to strength with jet aircraft aboard, with the first enormous US Navy 'supercarriers' emerging in the late 1950s, becoming the clearest signal of global power projection. In the other direction, the revolution in Vertical Take-Off and Landing gave smaller navies the tools to join the 'Carrier Club' and dramatically increase their military capabilities and global influence. It was enough to persuade the Soviet Union to overcome its scepticism and develop its own carriers and aircraft.

The difficult beginnings in the Korean War in the early 1950s gave way to the technological leaps that made jets truly at home on carriers. The way was paved for legendary aircraft such as the F-4 Phantom, Blackburn Buccaneer, F-14 Tomcat, and BAe Sea Harrier to make their mark in conflicts such as Vietnam, the Falklands, and the first Gulf War. Even though the classic jet age involved no carrier-to-carrier battles like those of World War Two, the importance of the carrier and its aircraft was never greater.

Matthew Willis
Editor

ABOVE: An F-8A Crusader prepares for a catapult launch from the world's first nuclear-powered supercarrier, USS *Enterprise*.
Author's collection

COVER ARTWORK BY ANDY HAY
www.flyingart.co.uk

CONTENTS

06

28

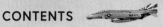

ISBN: 9781802829624
Editor: Matt Willis
Senior editor, specials: Roger Mortimer
Email: roger.mortimer@keypublishing.com
Cover Design: Steve Donovan
Design: SJmagic DESIGN SERVICES, India
Advertising Sales Manager: Sam Clark
Email: sam.clark@keypublishing.com
Tel: 01780 755131
Advertising Production: Becky Antoniades
Email: Rebecca.antoniades@ keypublishing.com

SUBSCRIPTION/MAIL ORDER
Key Publishing Ltd, PO Box 300, Stamford, Lincs, PE9 1NA
Tel: 01780 480404
Subscriptions email: subs@ keypublishing.com
Mail Order email: orders@keypublishing.com
Website: www.keypublishing.com/shop

PUBLISHING
Group CEO and Publisher: Adrian Cox
Published by
Key Publishing Ltd, PO Box 100, Stamford, Lincs, PE9 1XQ
Tel: 01780 755131 **Website:** www. keypublishing.com

PRINTING
Precision Colour Printing Ltd, Haldane, Halesfield 1, Telford, Shropshire. TF7 4QQ

DISTRIBUTION
Seymour Distribution Ltd, 2 Poultry Avenue, London, EC1A 9PU
Enquiries Line: 02074 294000.

THE FIRST JET CARRIER LANDING

It's certain that the first jet carrier landing took place in last months of 1945. What's less clear is where it took place, on which carrier, or the name of the pilot who can claim the honour. Matthew Willis explores an eight-decade old mystery.

According to the US Navy, the first jet carrier landing took place on November 6, 1945, aboard the escort carrier CVE 65 USS *Wake Island*, off San Diego, California. The pilot was Ensign Jake West of fighter squadron VF-41, and the aircraft, a Ryan FR-1 Fireball.

However, according to the Royal Navy, the first jet carrier landing took place on December 3, 1945, aboard the aircraft carrier HMS *Ocean*, in the English Channel. The pilot was Lieutenant Commander Eric 'Winkle' Brown, and the aircraft, a de Havilland Vampire.

But why are there competing claims? And which is correct?

To understand how this dispute came about, it's necessary to go back to 1945, and the situation with jets and aircraft carriers.

Fundamental problems

By the end of World War Two, it was increasingly apparent that the future of combat aircraft lay with the jet engine. The appearance of the Messerschmitt Me 262 over the skies of Europe in late 1944 showed that the current generation of propeller-driven aircraft could be made obsolete overnight. Only the Me 262's limited numbers and the fragility of the new technology prevented it from having a pivotal effect on the war. By the final Axis surrender in September 1945, air arms of three nations had introduced jet-powered aircraft into frontline service.

But jet aircraft in their current state were fundamentally unsuitable for operation from aircraft carriers. They had low acceleration, which was bad for take-offs and wave-offs; they had no propeller wash accelerating air over the wings and tail, enhancing low-speed flight for landing; and they had low endurance due to thirsty engines. It's true that they also had some advantages over piston aircraft – there was no torque from a propeller to cause control problems when the throttle was opened suddenly, and they tended to have better visibility forward and down due to the engine being behind the pilot – but in 1945, the problems far outweighed the benefits. It was even suggested that the arrival of jets might spell the end for aircraft carriers as we knew them.

Research agencies and navies began to look at the problems in earnest

and consider if they were soluble. But theory would only take things so far. To fully grasp the situation, somebody was going to have to try to land a jet on a carrier.

Compromise solution

When jet engines first emerged as a practical proposition in the early 1940s, the potential difficulties in adapting the technology to carrier use were quickly identified. The first jets were of relatively low power (the first practical Allied jet engine, the Power Jets W2B, developed around 1,500lb thrust) and acceleration from jet propulsion alone was low, while carrier flight depended on high power and acceleration both for take-off and landing. Carrier landing techniques with piston-engined aircraft had evolved towards using relatively high power on landing to overcome the drag of typically large high lift devices. The problem was particularly acute when it came to escort carriers, the small ships based on merchantman hulls, where short take-off and landing, and high acceleration were most needed.

For this reason, several of the first naval aircraft on the drawing board from mid-World War Two sought to combine the main advantages of the jet with the proven values of propeller aircraft. One example of these – in fact one of the few of these hybrid

aircraft to make it into production – was the Ryan FR-1 Fireball.

Design on the Fireball began in December 1942, and early the following year the US Navy formally expressed interest. It combined an airframe typical of a late-generation piston fighter, including a Wright R-1820-56 Cyclone in the nose, with a turbojet in the rear fuselage.

It was particularly attractive as it was small and light enough to be used from escort carriers. The piston engine was the same as that used in the Grumman FM-2, the specialist escort carrier fighter in use at the end of the war. Behind the pilot was a 1,600lb-thrust General Electric J31 turbojet, a US-developed engine derived from the British W2B.

The concept of the FR-1 was to operate like a piston-powered fighter with additional boost from the jet when needed – on take-off, climb, and in combat. At all other times, including landing, the jet would remain idle.

The combination increased complexity and weight, but it boosted endurance, payload and – in theory – reliability. The USN was so sure of the Fireball that it placed a production order before the prototype flew.

The first flight of the Fireball took place on June 25, 1944, on piston power alone. Carrier trials took place aboard USS *Charger* in January 1945, and demonstrated good landing and deck-handling.

At first glance, the Fireball looked like a propeller fighter. The only feature that looked particularly modern was its tricycle undercarriage, a first on a production aircraft for the USN. It was of relatively clean form, and its outer wings had a relatively new laminar-flow aerofoil, but its appearance was entirely conventional. From the outside, the only giveaway of its most innovative feature was the discreet jet nozzle in the extreme tail, and the even more subtle intakes in the wing root.

Performance was encouraging, considering the compromise inherent in the design. The FR-1's top speed was 404mph, 15mph faster than the Grumman F6F Hellcat, and it was more manoeuvrable too. Most importantly, in view of the 'Kamikaze' threat which beset the US Pacific Fleet at the time of the FR-1's trials, it offered an impressive climb rate, better than any piston-engined fighter.

In March 1945, the first frontline squadron to be assigned the Fireball – VF-66 – received its first aircraft and prepared for carrier qualification trials in a couple of months.

Pure jet

Unlike the US Navy, the British Fleet Air Arm (FAA) had not commissioned any combat aircraft with jet power before September 1944, though several had been considered and rejected. Guided by the Royal Aircraft Establishment, the UK's aeronautical research centre, the FAA decided that only pure jet aircraft had good enough performance for the future.

In April 1945, Supermarine, responsible for the famous Spitfire and its naval counterpart the Seafire, offered the FAA a naval version of a land-based interceptor then in development. The FAA debated the virtues of the Supermarine fighter for several months, but time was pressing, and the service needed **»**

LEFT: Ryan FR-1 taking off from USS *Wake Island* in late 1945, entering a starboard turn to clear the path for the next aircraft. The undercarriage is already mostly retracted. Author's collection

experience with jet aircraft. As a short term measure, the Navy purchased a small number of de Havilland Vampire jet fighters.

The Vampire was a lightweight interceptor developed for the RAF, powered by a Halford H.1 turbojet (later built by de Havilland as the Ghost). It first flew in September 1943 and the first frontline squadron would begin to receive aircraft in March 1946.

The FAA began flying the Vampire in 1945, receiving the third prototype LZ551/G. This was test-flown at RAE Farnborough, and in August was partially 'navalised' – modified to allow deck-landing.

Before physical deck landing trials of a jet aircraft could be considered,

a great deal of preparation had to be done at Farnborough and the naval air station at Arbroath.

A series of trials of the arrester gear took place throughout October and November 1945, leading to slight modifications to the hook, as well as offering valuable information as to how to best carry out the deck landings.

The pilot selected was, perhaps inevitable, Lieutenant Commander Eric Melrose Brown, best known by his nickname 'Winkle.'

LZ551/G was powered by a Halford H.1A offering 2,700lb thrust. It had been fitted with an A-frame arrester hook, attached to the wing trailing edge root either side of the fuselage, and stowed in a fairing above the jetpipe. The hook had to fall through

the jet exhaust flow every time it was deployed so much testing was required to ensure the hook could tolerate this without weakening.

Deck trials and tribulations

The pilots of VF-66 took their Fireballs to sea for the first time in May 1945. Three of the fighters were sent to carry out carrier suitability trials for the type aboard CV-4 USS *Ranger*. The results were unfortunately mixed. Although demonstrating no major flaws in handling, during the three days of the trials, two of the three FR-1s were rendered unserviceable, one suffering a collapsed nosewheel and the other hitting the crash barrier.

This set back the programme, and probably contributed significantly to VF-66's failure to attain operational status by the time the war in the Pacific came to an end at the

beginning of September. The truth was that the Fireball was somewhat fragile for a carrier type.

Ryan had made a significant achievement when it created a twin-engined aircraft with two different fuel systems that weighed in at almost 4,000lb less than the Grumman Hellcat. But this was, to an extent, achieved at the expense of durability. The wing was delicate, and cracking became a problem in service. The undercarriage in particular was too fragile to survive the kind of sustained abuse that was typical to carrier operation. This was exacerbated by the arrester hook being located under the fuselage; the jetpipe meant it could not be fitted in the usual place at the tail, but this led to a sharp nose-down pitch when the hook caught a wire.

The end of the war removed the need for the Fireball, and most of the 700 aircraft ordered were cancelled. The US Navy received only 66.

VF-66 transferred its aircraft to VF-41, which embarked on USS *Wake Island* on November 5 for carrier qualification.

The following day, Ensign West was in the pattern to land when his R-1820 began to lose power. Although the J31 was not normally used during landing at all, West realised he had

a choice – ditch, or try for the deck with his 'spare' engine. Thinking quickly, he started up the J31, which gave him just enough power to reach the deck. The FR-1's hook snagged the last wire, and the nose ran into the barrier. It wasn't the cleanest landing, but West was down safe.

Planned attack

Geoffrey Cooper was an engineer with the Royal Aircraft Establishment in 1945 who had taken part in many carrier aircraft evaluations. He was assigned to the RAE team aboard *Ocean* to observe

the trials with the Vampire planned for December 1945. Cooper's job was to check the accelerometers fitted to the aircraft and change the recorders after each landing. On December 3, it looked as though the weather would not co-operate, but Winkle decided to try anyway – to the surprise of those on board.

Cooper recalled: "By that time we were operating in the Channel. And so, we were south of the Isle of Wight, and we were steaming there, on *Ocean*, waiting for Winkle to come, and it was piped aboard ship that the Vampire was delayed at **»**

ABOVE: Crowds of crew and VIPs rush to congratulate Lieutenant Commander Brown on his successful first jet deck landing aboard HMS *Ocean* on December 3, 1945. Author's collection

LEFT: Lieutenant Commander Brown poses for the camera with Vampire LZ551/G after the first successful jet deck landing, even as maintainers ready the aircraft for its first carrier take-off. Key collection

on pushing the throttle forward, for him to gain flying speed again. The deck was completely clear of all, of anything, no barrier or anything, to give him enough room because he only had 760 feet of flight deck.

"He'd already had plenty of practice with this, because he'd had the practice at Arbroath as well as at Farnborough, for batting in. He approached normally – circle round anti-clockwise, come in on the port side, circle in, and come down from about 500 feet, a gradual approach – up a bit, down a bit, cut!

"And given the cut signal, he did not stop the engine, that was one thing about it, he kept the engine running at low revs. And he came in, perfectly on the centreline, dead in line all the way through, straight in and made a perfect landing. The only thing was, he landed a little bit up-deck, and the wire flipped up and damaged the flaps. These were examined on board ship – I think we did two more flights with the damaged flap, but we carried no fuel on board ship, so he had to fly back to Ford. So, he went back and had about four inches of flap cut off. I think we did 14 landings all told. On the subsequent flights, after each three or four landings he had to go back to Ford to tank up again. Although the first night he stayed on board, with the plane lashed down to the deck – but there was no accommodation for him! It was all occupied by all

ABOVE AND RIGHT: Two photographs by famed aviation photographer Charles E Brown, of Vampire LZ551/G taking off from HMS *Ocean* during the three-day deck trial period in December 1945.
Author's collection

Ford, I don't know for what purpose, so we started steaming back to harbour. We had just turned round to come back to Portsmouth when there was a whistle and a roar, and a Vampire flew at deck level down the starboard side, round the port side, and circled. So, on board ship, it was 'belay the last pipe, action stations! Hands to flying stations!' So, we turned round again, into wind,

meanwhile Winkle was circling. And then he was brought in by the batsman – the deck landing control officer – flagging him.

"Well, it was all an immense amount of anxiety. Of course, we had all the barriers down so that if he missed a wire he could fly through, but one of the problems was he had to throttle back to land, and if he missed a wire it took a long time,

these VIPs, and people like me, and photographers. He had to sleep on a wardroom couch, but that didn't bother him.

"It took two or three days, closer to three days. He was so accomplished at deck landing; you couldn't fault him on that at all. He used to ask us sometimes, which wire did we want picked up? But he didn't ask us before with the Vampire!"

Who was first?

The deck landing by 'Winkle' had been planned over months – West's was planned in seconds. They were almost mirror-opposite achievements, one the result of methodical planning and leaving nothing to chance, the other a brilliant bit of improvisation. Both were undoubtedly brilliant pieces of flying. But which can be said to be the first jet carrier landing?

West's landing obviously took place before Winkle's. But there is some doubt that it was the first to be carried out *under jet power alone*.

Squadron Leader Michael Biggs wrote that: "According to US Naval Historian Norman Polmar, the USN was embarrassed by this claim as the investigation of the incident shows that only a partial power failure of the piston engine occurred, and the emergency landing was made using a

combination of the residual power in the piston engine augmented by use of the jet engine. It was pointed out that the Fireball with a dead engine, windmilling propeller, undercarriage and flaps down could not have made it to the deck on 1,600lbs thrust."

Polmar himself added: "it is believed the piston engine did not lose its full power," and described Brown's landing as "the first true jet carrier landings."

It seems likely that West may have retained some power from the failing R-1820. The air start procedure for the J31 took 30 seconds, and it seems unlikely that a FR-1 in 'dirty' condition could have glided for long enough – even if the

small jet was enough by itself. Some accounts suggest that West feathered his propeller – necessary if the R-1820 was shut down completely – but this is not supported by primary evidence.

So, at best it is not proven that West's landing was the first entirely under jet power. It was, however, clearly the first carrier landing to involve jet power. Moreover, it should be celebrated as a feat of carrier aviation whether or not it was strictly the first.

Winkle Brown carried out the first confirmed deck landing under jet power alone, and the first take-off too. The HMS *Ocean* trials were the foundation on which postwar British naval aviation was built.

EARLY STEPS TO CARRIER JETS

By the late 1940s, the aircraft carrier with piston-engined air-groups had reached a peak of sophistication. The arrival of the jet threatened to render all that development useless, perhaps even obsolete. The early postwar period showed that jets were the future – but the road was long and troubled.

The flight of the first British jet aircraft in 1941 would introduce some of the biggest challenges in the development of carrier aviation. By the end of World War Two, it was apparent that the jet engine promised a remarkable step forward in performance, but operating jet aircraft at sea, with their low acceleration, lack of propwash-generated lift, and lack of endurance, would have to be tackled if carriers were not to become obsolete.

The last generation of propeller-driven carrier aircraft proved that their performance could be every bit as good as their land based equivalents – which was essential if they were to operate within range of land-based aircraft.

From late World War Two to the mid-1950s, both the USN and the FAA pursued unconventional solutions against the possibility that the carrier did prove to be untenable in the jet age. This included vertical take-off aircraft such as the British Fairey VTO,

a proposed rocket-powered delta for launch from 'zero-length' platforms, and the American Convair XFY-1 Pogo and Lockheed XFV, a pair of turboprop-driven tail sitters. Another avenue pursued independently on both sides of the Atlantic was the 'flexible deck' – a cushioned flight deck that allowed catapult-launched aircraft with no undercarriage to land safely.

In the event, conventional aircraft proved practical, and the experiments were ended.

At the beginning of World War Two, four navies actively operated carriers – the British, US, Japanese, and French navies. France lagged behind the other three and did not maintain carrier operations after signing an armistice with Germany in 1940. Carriers were acquired around the end of the war in Europe but short-lived plans for a new fleet carrier that could operate jets was cancelled in 1950.

At the end of the war, the defeat of Japan and the complete disbandment of its armed forces, also put that country out of the

carrier aviation arena. Many of the wartime Allied nations were interested in acquiring and operating carriers but it would be many years before they were capable of operating jets.

This left the UK and US as the sole major carrier powers into the 1950s, and chiefly responsible for developing the state-of-the-art in the field.

First principles

The first jet landings on HMS *Ocean* were described by the pioneering pilot, Lieutenant Commander Eric 'Winkle' Brown, as a "direct and very successful attack on the problem of deck-landing jet-propelled aircraft." However, he confirmed the Admiralty's feeling that the Vampire would not be suitable for full carrier operations. This delayed the Fleet Air Arm gaining jet aircraft in squadron service while it waited for more appropriate types to be developed.

Nevertheless, Vampires continued to be

BELOW: A de Havilland Vampire settling onto the trial 'flexible deck' at the RAE Farnborough in 1947–48. The flexible deck was intended to eliminate the weight and bulk of undercarriage to increase fuel capacity on early short-range jets. Royal Navy via US Naval Institute

used to 'directly attack' the problem. LZ551/G, the first pure jet aircraft to land on an aircraft carrier, was used in further trials the following year. The Fleet Air Arm (FAA) ordered 20 Vampire fighters, which were built to Sea Vampire Mk.20 standard, with arrester hooks and strengthened undercarriages. They would operate extensively over the next few years to gain further data on jet carrier operations.

A Carrier Trials Unit was formed, and two of its pilots made over 200 deck landings on HMS *Illustrious* during Exercise Sunrise in 1948. This experience was invaluable in preparing the Fleet Air Arm's pilots for the switch to jet fighters.

The propeller hangs on

The advantages of a propeller were difficult for carrier navies to dispense with in the early days of jet flight. The wash from the blades accelerated air over part of the wing and tail surfaces, increasing lift and control relative to forward speed. Aircraft with propellers were also better able to cruise economically. Efforts were therefore made to retain the benefits of the propeller with the performance of a jet.

One example was the mixed-power aircraft, such as the Ryan FR-1 as described in the previous chapter. The concept was popular with the USN in the early days of jet development but only the FR-1 entered service, and only in small numbers. During the carrier qualification trials where Ensign Jake West had become the first pilot to land using jet power, VF-41 experienced numerous undercarriage failures and only two-thirds of its pilots completed sufficient carrier landings to qualify. »

ABOVE: A scale research model of the Fairey VTO (Vertical Take-Off) interceptor developed through the late 1940s. The VTO was intended to take off from a 'zero-length' launcher on a ship. Trials took place from a ship in Cardigan Bay and Woomera, Australia. Although the VTO project did not reach the full-size test stage, it led to the Fairey Delta 1 research aircraft.
Author's collection

ABOVE: This image of DH Sea Vampire F.20 VV150 of 702 Squadron was taken aboard HMS *Theseus* during a naval training exercise in July 1950 as part of the Royal Navy's trials into carrier jet operations. The Vampires share deck space with the Seafires of 1832 RNVR NAS. The trolley at lower left is to facilitate manoeuvring the Vampire below decks, as it had non-folding wings.
Author's collection

Ryan attempted to address structural weaknesses but during a later carrier qualification period aboard HMS *Badoeng Strait* in early 1947, fewer than half the pilots managed to complete enough take-offs and landings to qualify. The type was withdrawn completely within months.

Aware of the limited shelf-life of the FR-1, Ryan considered developments of the aircraft. The Model 29 replaced the piston engine with a General Electric XT31 turboprop, retaining the J31 turbojet in the rear fuselage.

RIGHT: An exploded diagram of the Ryan FR-1 Fireball mixed-power interceptor. The J31 turbojet can be seen between the aft and middle fuselage sections.
Author's collection

This increased performance from 404mph to 497mph and simplified the fuel supply – jet and piston engines used different fuels – while retaining a greater range than a purely piston powered aircraft. A prototype was converted from a production FR-1, and the US Navy's Bureau of Aeronautics (BuAer) allocated the designation XF2R-1.

The XF2R-1 first flew in November 1946. Even the navy appeared to consider it more as a flying laboratory to assess the turboprop than as a future combat aircraft.

Ryan offered the Model 34, a further developed version with a swept wing, which it claimed would be capable of 651mph – similar to a North American F-86A Sabre. BuAer concluded that the stalling speed would be excessive, and here the line of Ryan naval fighters ended.

An ambitious project from France for a carrier-based strike and anti-submarine aircraft was commissioned from Bréguet in 1947, for a still-born carrier project. The Br 960 Vultur had an Armstrong Siddeley Mamba turboprop in the nose and a Rolls-Royce Nene turbojet in the rear fuselage. The first prototype displayed poor handling qualities when it first flew in 1951 and was overweight to such an extent that the turbojet had to be kept running at all times. A second prototype showed improvement, but the new carrier had been cancelled and the Br 960 died with it, though the design was evolved into an anti-submarine aircraft.

Turboprop promise

While the mixed-power aircraft was a dead end, both the USN and the FAA pursued the pure turboprop, in which a turbine engine uses jet thrust to turn a propeller as well as the compressor stages of the engine.

The turboprop offered an increase in performance for strike aircraft

RIGHT: Ryan XF2R-1, known informally as the Dark Shark, in flight in January 1947. The XF2R-1 swapped its predecessor's R-1820 piston engine for a General Electric T31 turboprop but retained the J31 turbojet in the rear fuselage.
Author's collection

BELOW: VP120, one of six prototypes of the Westland Wyvern strike fighter, and the only one to be fitted with the Rolls-Royce Clyde turboprop, in 1949, around the time of its first flight. The Clyde was the favoured engine but was cancelled, so production aircraft were fitted with the Armstrong Siddeley Python.
Author's collection

without all the disadvantages of pure thrust engines. While the acceleration of turboprops was lower than piston engines, it was better than turbojets, and turboprops were also more economical.

In the UK, a large, powerful strike fighter under development by Westland in late World War Two, with a 3,000hp Rolls-Royce Eagle engine, was examined for suitability for a turboprop powerplant. An engine from Armstrong-Siddeley, the Python, was one possibility and another was Rolls-Royce's Clyde. This aircraft became the Wyvern.

Examples powered by all three engines were flown, the piston-engined version in 1945 and the turboprop-powered versions in 1949. The Eagle and the Clyde were subsequently cancelled leaving the Python as the only possibility.

In the US, BuAer approached the Douglas Aircraft Company for a strike fighter powered by one of several new turboprops under development. As in the UK, most of the proposed engines were cancelled, and Douglas was restricted to the Allison XT40-A2 – a somewhat complex powerplant comprising two turbine units side by side, the drive united in a gearbox to drive contra-rotating propellers on a single axis. This became the A2D Skyshark. It first flew in 1950.

Both these aircraft suffered significant development problems, and neither were in a position to enter service until 1953. In the event, the Skyshark never attained frontline service.

The turboprop was entertained for naval combat aircraft as an interim solution before pure thrust engines could dependably power carrier strike aircraft with sufficient range and payload. As it turned out, all the turboprop carrier aircraft in development in the late 1940s, whether pure turboprop or mixed power, suffered lengthy delays and complex development problems. Only the Wyvern entered frontline service and that was beaten into service by two pure jet aircraft.

However, the turboprop was rather more successful in the anti-submarine role. During World War Two, the FAA relied heavily on carrier-based aircraft for anti-submarine warfare (ASW), and this had reached a sophisticated state by the end of the war, with technology such as sonobuoys and radar for detecting both submerged and surfaced aircraft. World War Two showed that the threats to sea-lines of communication from submarines were such that dedicated anti-submarine aircraft with a range of weapons including homing torpedoes would be necessary. The turboprop offered the endurance and economy that was needed. From a specification in 1945, the Fairey Gannet, powered by a twin, coupled turboprop – the Armstrong Siddeley Twin Mamba – emerged, entering service in 1954.

The French Navy came to the same conclusion in the early 1950s, and »

First-generation specialists

From the mid-1940s, the main carrier navies commissioned a series of jet carrier fighters, even before it was clear that the problems associated with jet power could be solved.

The US was in the fortunate position of plentiful funds to pursue a series of potential avenues of development, both in concepts and individual classes of aircraft. The USN sponsored Westinghouse to develop jet engines for naval aircraft, and as an insurance policy, in 1947 paid for a licensing agreement for Pratt & Whitney to build the 5,000lb-thrust British Rolls-Royce Nene. BuAer

asked Bréguet to adapt its stillborn Bréguet Br 960 Vultur. The second prototype Vultur was modified with the turbojet removed as the Br 965, serving as 'proof of concept,' and a more substantial redesign resulted in the Rolls-Royce Dart-powered Alizé, which joined frontline squadrons in 1957.

also pursued both the mixed-power interceptor and pure jet designs.

The first pure jet design for the US Navy was the McDonnell FH-1 Phantom – not to be confused with the later F-4 Phantom II from the same manufacturer. The original Phantom was a conventional straight-wing design, considered rather safe and unimpressive by BuAer, powered by a Westinghouse J30 turbojet. This was of the more efficient axial-flow design than the British engines of the time, but difficulties with its development delayed the FH-1's flight until the end of January 1945, when it demonstrated a top speed of just over 500mph.

By this time, mock dogfights between US Navy Grumman Bearcats and US Air Force Lockheed Shooting Stars starkly highlighted the superiority of jets, leading BuAer to set up a competition for a fighter with a more impressive performance, hoping for 550–560mph.

Submissions were received from North American Aviation (NAA), Chance Vought, and McDonnell.

Grumman later made an unsolicited submission. The USN selected the NAA aircraft as the FJ-1 Fury (not to be confused with the later FJ-2/3/4 Fury series derived from the Sabre).

The Fury was developed from the NAA P-51H Mustang, with similar laminar flow wings. It's generally thought of as an also-ran today, but at the time of its first flight in 1947, it was one of the fastest fighters in the world, at 552mph, and had a better climb performance than the US Air Force's Lockheed F-80. It was in service quickly, with the first squadron formed in March 1948. Its meagre reputation is chiefly indication of how quickly jets were advancing at the time.

The US Navy also ordered a small number of the Chance Vought design as the F6U Pirate, a rather ungainly, snub-nosed machine, because it had an innovative afterburner to boost the thrust of its Westinghouse J34 jet. Unfortunately, the afterburner failed to work well, and the Pirate's performance was lower than existing piston-engined fighters. A mere 30 were built and it never joined a first-line squadron.

Grumman's day fighter emerged as the Nene-powered F9F Panther, by far the most successful early US naval jet. McDonnell developed the FH-1 into the F2H Banshee, which found its niche as a capable all-weather fighter.

The British Fleet Air Arm quickly rejected mixed-power as a solution and went straight for pure jet aircraft, although they were later to start than the USN. Supermarine was developing a jet interceptor based on the wing of the Spiteful, a piston fighter intended to replace the Spitfire. This would be powered by a Nene and became the Attacker, the FAA's first frontline jet, joining 800 Squadron in 1951. It had a relatively impressive performance for a straight-winged jet at 590mph, but it was otherwise disappointing and was supplanted within a few years

by the rival Hawker Sea Hawk. This was another Nene-powered straight-wing design of unusually clean form. It had a similar top speed to the Attacker but was otherwise much more capable.

The last first-generation jet to join the FAA was the de Havilland Sea Venom, a night/all-weather fighter acquired as a stop-gap as plans for a more advanced all-weather fighter had hit delays.

The Sea Venom was closely related to the Vampire, mainly differing with a new, thinner wing. It had an airborne-interception radar in the nose and a side-by-side two-seat cockpit to accommodate the pilot and the radar operator. It was powered by a DH Ghost engine of just under 5,000lb thrust.

The French navy approached the industry in 1946 for an interceptor to operate from its projected new carrier. Prototypes were ordered from Nord Aviation, SNCAC and Arsenal, and all featured a moderately swept wing. The prototypes all flew in 1949, but the cancellation of France's new carrier the following year left their future in doubt. All three designs suffered troubled development culminating in fatal crashes during test flying. The difficulty of the programmes and the cancellation of the PA-28 carrier meant that the Aéronavale decided to purchase the British Sea Venom, which would be licence-built as the SNCASE Aquilon.

The immediate problems of operating jets from aircraft carriers had been addressed, in time for the first major war after the transition from propeller to jet began – Korea.

ABOVE: The challenges of introducing jets meant that scenes like this one, aboard HMS *Centaur* in 1954–55, were common until the late 1950s, where new Hawker Sea Hawk jets share a deck with Hawker Sea Fury fighter-bombers and Grumman Avenger anti-submarine aircraft. This led to inconveniences for carriers such as carrying two different kinds of aviation fuel.
Author's collection

LEFT: Prototype Arsenal VG 90 F-WFDE demonstrating its 22° swept wing. The Aéronavale tested the VG 90 among several state-of-the-art carrier combat aircraft for its postwar carrier programme, but the prototypes all suffered significant difficulties and British aircraft were acquired instead.
Author's collection

CARRIER JETS OVER KOREA

When war broke out on the Korean peninsula in 1950, involving the nascent United Nations, carrier aviation with jets had barely begun. Yet despite all the limitations of early jets, and the challenges brought by revolutionary swept-wing fighters, the jet-powered naval aircraft soon proved their worth.

I n May 1948, the first USN squadron operating jets became operational, when VF-17A qualified for carrier operations with the McDonnell FH-1 Phantom aboard USS *Saipan*. A mere two years later, jets were an integral part of the USN's complement of combat aircraft and were about to go into action over Korea.

The Royal Navy's Fleet Air Arm would not operate jets in the Korean War. Although the FAA introduced its first jet fighter, the Supermarine Attacker, to first-line service the year after the war began, these aircraft would remain in home waters with the larger carriers. The light-fleet carriers operated by the RN and its Commonwealth counterparts in Korean operations did not operate jets and could not do so routinely until they were modernised. When North Korea started deploying jets, this largely restricted FAA

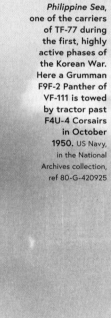

BELOW: The flight deck of the USS *Philippine Sea*, one of the carriers of TF-77 during the first, highly active phases of the Korean War. Here a Grumman F9F-2 Panther of VF-111 is towed by tractor past F4U-4 Corsairs in October 1950. US Navy, in the National Archives collection, ref 80-G-420925

aircraft to ground attack and tactical reconnaissance.

The USN on the other hand brought fleet carriers to Korean waters and would operate Grumman F9F Panthers and McDonnell F2H Banshees from the outset as a matter of routine. USN and Marine squadrons also operated naval jets from shore bases, including the Douglas F3D night fighter.

First exchanges

After World War Two, when Korea was liberated from Japan, it was divided along the 38th parallel into zones occupied by the US in the south, and the USSR in the north. Negotiations to reunite the country

under a single government failed, and two states were set up, the Democratic People's Republic of Korea in the north and the Republic of Korea in the south, generally referred to simply as North Korea and South Korea.

Most thought the solution, crude though it was, had brought stability. The USN carrier USS *Boxer* visited Inchon in early 1950 to show the flag, and a flypast of Grumman Panther jets, plus Vought Corsair and Douglas Skyraider propeller planes, was undoubtedly an impressive indication of the US's willingness to support South Korea.

It was a shock to western militaries when North Korea invaded South Korea on June 25, 1950. The United Nations condemned the act and demanded a ceasefire. North Korea ignored the plea, and the UN authorised military action to defend South Korea.

Airbases were available to UN forces in South Korea. Nevertheless, aircraft carriers proved vital to the UN effort. With Korea being a peninsula, with thousands of miles of coastline, aircraft launched from carriers were able to access targets deep into enemy territory.

The North Korean Air Force should not have been a cause for particular concern. Though it was much more powerful than the South Korean equivalent, it was small by the standards of the major military powers and made up entirely of Soviet World War Two-era piston-engined types.

On the declaration of war, USN and RN forces in the Far East moved towards Korean waters where they joined Task Force 77 (TF 77) under the US Seventh Fleet. In July, USS *Valley Forge* arrived on station off the west coast, becoming the first carrier involved in the conflict with jets as part of its air group. Aboard *Valley Forge* was Carrier Air Group 5 (CAG 5) with VF-51 and VF-52's F9F Panthers as well as VA-55's Skyraiders, and the Corsairs of VF-53 and VF-54. USS *Philippine Sea* arrived the following month, with CAG 11's two squadrons of F9F Panthers, VF-111 and VF-112, as well as two squadrons of Corsairs and one of Skyraiders.

The first ever combat operation by carrier jets took place on July 3, 1950. This was a strike against an airfield south of Pyongyang, British carrier aircraft had attacked that morning. Eight VF-51 Panthers launched from *Valley Forge*, planning to arrive just before the propeller aircraft, to destroy enemy aircraft on the ground and prevent any that got airborne from interfering with the strike. When they reached Haeju, however, the Panther pilots found that the

alarm had been raised and Yakovlev fighters were desperately scrambling. Two cool-headed naval pilots slotted in behind Yaks that were taking off, and their four 20mm cannon made short work of the North Korean aircraft.

The next day involved a strike on a bridge, something that would become a staple target of carrier aircraft.

As the Corsairs and Skyraiders arrived the jets moved off, their main job done, to attack any valuable »

ABOVE: Grumman F9F-2 #123438 strikes the barrier on USS *Philippine Sea* on October 19, 1950, after returning from a combat mission over Korea. Barrier strikes by jets often ended up in damage to aircraft parked forward as the steel cables typically sliced the undercarriage off instead of bringing the aircraft to a stop. US Navy, in the National Archives collection, ref 80-G-420958

LEFT: Grumman F9F-2 Panthers of VF-51 manoeuvred aboard USS *Valley Forge* during the first weeks of operations over Korea in July 1950. The carrier's deck tractors were soon found to be inadequate for routine handling of jets, as they were built for smaller aircraft that took off and landed less frequently. Naval History and Heritage Command, ref NH 96978

targets in the surrounding area that might present themselves.

In the second half of July, *Valley Forge* instigated a routine of launching a 32 propeller-plane strike followed by two 12-aircraft jet sweeps. Later, this was adjusted to a 12–16 propeller aircraft strike followed by an eight aircraft jet sweep. A four-aircraft CAP of F9Fs was also maintained over the task force.

The sweeps were essentially armed reconnaissance sorties, attacking targets of opportunity and bringing back information on enemy dispositions. On July 18, 1950, for example once four divisions of F9Fs were airborne and formed up, two divisions headed up the coast to Wonsan, with the other two heading inland to Pyongyang. The propeller aircraft, meanwhile, were providing direct support to amphibious landings at Pohang.

The Wonsan aircraft strafed a hangar and other targets, and reconnoitred the Wonsan oil refinery, noting that despite several raids by US Air Force B-29s in recent days, it looked totally undamaged.

The Pyongyang aircraft found an inviting target of two rows of single-engined aircraft neatly lined up, closely spaced. The F9Fs each made two strafing runs up and down the aircraft, then strafed a train until the boiler blew.

A second Pyongyang strike following close after the first reported

LEFT: A reconnaissance photo of the American advance following the landings at Inchon in September 1950. Burning, wrecked North Korean T-34 tanks can be seen to right and left while US tanks and infantry move along the road. USN aircraft provided close support to US ground forces during and after the landings.
Author's collection

more aircraft destroyed on the ground, and then ranged around for targets of opportunity to strafe and hit with their bombs, tearing up rail track and damaging tank-carrying rail cars. A rail bridge was then bombed, one span being knocked out.

When the Panther pilots returned to *Valley Forge* and made their report on the oil refinery, the mission planners responded swiftly. A raid made up of Corsairs and Skyraiders was armed and dispatched in the early evening and attacked the target with rockets and bombs. The refinery was utterly wrecked, and an estimated 12,000 tons of refined oil was destroyed. The smoke column could be seen 60 miles away.

No enemy aircraft were encountered in the air during any of the CAG's sorties that day.

The following day, July 19, 1950, the CAG's F9Fs took part in a raid further north. Again, the Panthers operated independently from the propeller planes, carrying out sweeps to the airfields at Yonpo, Sondok and Kanko. Parked Yaks and Ilyushin Il-10s were spotted at the first two, and they were comprehensively shot up. Lieutenant (jg) Heiderer of VF-52 crashed into the sea during a catapult launch due to his engine failing at the worst possible moment. He was picked up, unharmed, by the plane guard helicopter.

According to *Valley Forge*'s captain, that day: "The most spectacular

damage occurred at Inchon. Attacked by first one group of F9Fs and then by the other, seven huge oil storage tanks and two small ones were destroyed by burning. Fires started by 20mm ammunition blazed fiercely with towering flames and black smoke extending thousands of feet into the clouds."

After the USS *Philippine Sea* joined TF 77 in August, she replaced the British HMS *Triumph* which went back to operating within a Royal Navy squadron. *Philippine Sea*'s Commanding Officer reported that that month, CAG 11's "jet planes were used to sweep airfields and lines of communication." On August 9 alone, four locomotives were destroyed and a further 11 were damaged.

In USS *Philippine Sea*'s first month of operation, three F9F's were lost, one in combat and two to accidents. One pilot, Ensign Curtis Smith of VF-112, was killed in combat.

The Pusan Pocket

The advance of North Korean forces seemed inexorable in July. The South Korean army withdrew south by the day, and the support of understrength and under-trained US units, hurriedly thrown into the conflict, did little to stem the advance. South Korean forces appeared on the brink of defeat.

By the end of August, KPA, the North Korean army, had overrun ❯❯

LEFT: A reconnaissance photograph of the island of Wolmi-do after heavy attacks by USN aircraft prior to the landings at Inchon in September 1950. A British Fairey Firefly is visible to the right of the large smoke column. Several fires burn ashore, and ships sunk in the harbour can be seen. Author's collection

BELOW: A Chinese People's Liberation Army Air Force MiG-15bis of the kind that first faced USN jets in November 1950 and displayed significantly better performance, though naval jets managed to shoot down several MiGs. Author's collection

ABOVE: A MiG-15bis during in-flight refuelling. This capability gave the MiG greater time to loiter and more time in the combat zone, an additional advantage over straight-wing USN jets, especially the F9F which was plagued by low endurance.
Author's collection

all but a square of territory at the southeastern corner of the peninsula around the port of Pusan, known as the 'Pusan Pocket.' The UN strategy was to withdraw behind a defensive perimeter and build up forces for a counteroffensive.

The immediate priority, however, was to defend the Pocket. If it could not be held, the war would be lost. Several heavy KPA assaults had to be repulsed in early August.

This led to a huge demand for navy planes to carry out direct close support of army units. At first, this proved difficult, mostly through technical problems with communication between air and ground. The US Navy and the US Air Force conducted close-support

in very different ways, while use of different maps by the different services and poor radio discipline by aircrew, also contributed to the difficulties. The situation did nothing for inter-service harmony in the fractious atmosphere following the retreat to the perimeter.

Yet more strain was applied to the carriers when the US Air Force withdrew all its aircraft out of the Pocket to Japan in mid-August.

Still, once initial complications were ironed out, the USN's close support provision became increasingly effective. The jets though played relatively little part in these operations. Experience quickly showed that propeller planes were far more effective in the role.

On July 25, a 'Free Navy Opportunity Area' was established outside the Pusan Pocket where Navy aircraft could maintain a presence all day and safely attack any target identified without fear of hitting friendly forces, the priority being transport and communications. The arrival of US Marines to help defend the Pocket on August 7 helped the close-support problems, as Marines and USN squadrons were accustomed to working with each other.

Unfortunately, during this period several unnecessary attacks on civilians were made. An order that groups of more than 8-10 people should be considered enemy troops led to agricultural workers in a field being strafed, and a pottery factory was misidentified as an ammunition dump and suffered the same fate. The rules of engagement were adjusted as a result. Once again, the jets were typically engaged on free-ranging sweeps, focussed on airfields, and road and rail targets, but as often as not, they had difficulty identifying appropriate targets and were often puzzled by what they saw on the ground.

Attempts to break out of the Pocket in August failed. A massive KPA offensive on August 26 almost broke the UN lines, but cost the KPA dearly, as the UN air forces held almost total air superiority.

RIGHT: Snowy weather aboard USS Essex during January 1952. One advantage jets demonstrated was a reduced susceptibility to cold compared with propeller aircraft, and jets were even used to clear flight decks of snow and ice. Here, McDonnell F2H Banshees (the two nearest jets) share space with Grumman F9Fs (on the deck edge, centre-top) and Vought F4Us. US Navy, in the National Archives collection, ref 80-G-437710

LEFT: The specialist photographic reconnaissance version of the Grumman Panther, the F9F-5P. The camera port in the side of the nose is clearly visible. The unarmed F9F-5P was a mainstay of USN intelligence-gathering in the Korean War, sometimes flown by US Marine squadrons as seen here. Author's collection

the same equipment and practices. The much increased size and performance of aircraft had *Philippine Sea*'s captain complaining that his aircraft were "literally chewing up the deck at an alarming rate."

The number of specialised sub-types had ballooned too – often in addition to a 'standard' type, specialised versions for night operations and photographic reconnaissance were operated by the same squadron, increasing the spares requirements and the specialist knowledge of maintenance and armament crew.

One problem that had not been foreseen was the toll on flight deck tractors, especially with the vastly more frequent deck-spotting activities caused by the jets' short endurance. Another unforeseen »

LEFT AND BELOW: A flight of three F9F-5s of VF-23 flying over the sea from USS *Essex* in the squadron's third deployment to Korea, flying its second type from its third carrier during that conflict. Despite the peaceful nature of the photographs, the squadron was heavily engaged, flying joint operations with the US Air Force, striking targets around Pyongyang, the capital of North Korea. Author's collection

Who is the enemy?

The early UN carrier operations were marred by a high number of deck accidents, which affected jets worst of all.

The problem was that in the short time since World War Two, the increased size and performance of carrier aircraft had made carrier operations a significantly more complex business, while the carriers themselves had changed little.

The captain of USS *Philippine Sea* lamented: "It is not difficult to appreciate the complexity of flight deck operations requiring constant spotting and re-spotting of the nine different types of aircraft comprising this ship's air group. The flight deck operations of World War Two, if compared to the present operations, would seem most elementary."

The carriers themselves were essentially the same as they had been at the end of the Pacific war, with

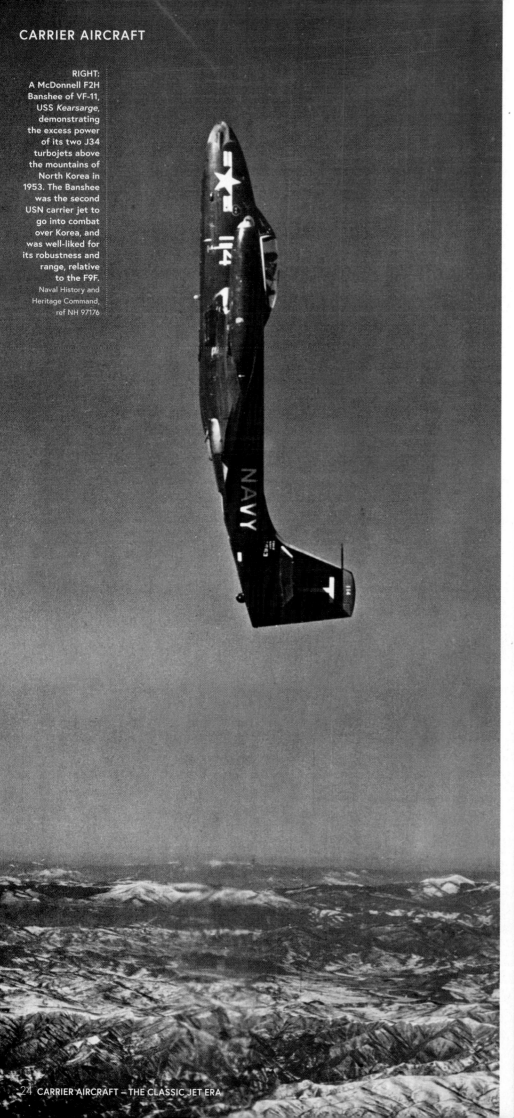

RIGHT:
A McDonnell F2H Banshee of VF-11, USS *Kearsarge*, demonstrating the excess power of its two J34 turbojets above the mountains of North Korea in 1953. The Banshee was the second USN carrier jet to go into combat over Korea, and was well-liked for its robustness and range, relative to the F9F.
Naval History and Heritage Command, ref NH 97176

problem with Anti-Aircraft (AA) gunsights was caused by jets running their engines up on deck, as they could be damaged by the jet blast.

Operating jets was also putting unprecedented strain on the carriers' machinery. In September, *Philippine Sea*'s captain reported that: "The nearly continuous operations with the high and varying speeds required for jet operations, demanded a high performance from engineering personnel and machinery. Full boiler power was required for a large part of the time, preventing underway maintenance." While he concluded that "Performance of men and machinery was generally excellent," continual running repairs were required to keep boilers functioning. He added that "evidence of fatigue has been noticeable" in flight deck and hangar deck crew, who were required to spend 16–20 hours on the job every day, in no small part due to the additional workload imposed by the Panthers.

But worst of all was the all-too frequent crash on deck. All aircraft types were affected, but

the consequences always seemed to be worst when jets were involved. On September 29, 1950, an F9F crashed through all *Philippine Sea*'s barriers and hit the aircraft parked forward, damaging 12 machines, and injuring five men.

Philippine Sea's captain reported: "On 14 November, an F9F jet crashed through all three Davis barriers when a pitching deck caused the hook to break on striking the ramp, and the landing gear failed as a result of the ensuing hard landing. The fire which started after the plane crashed into other aircraft parked forward of the barriers was quickly extinguished, thanks to a splendid performance on the part of fire-fighting personnel and equipment."

He added that "...accidents of this type can be expected to reoccur until a successor to the Davis barrier is developed which will positively arrest jet aircraft with damaged landing gear."

According to legend, the preponderance of crashes on deck, especially at a time when combat losses were light, had one member

of TF 77 inquiring "Just who is the enemy?"

On the other hand, some advantages came to be felt when the winter cold arrived in November. Piston engines took twice as long to warm up, while jets were unaffected. On occasions when the carrier sailed through a snowstorm, two F9Fs were taxied up the deck, 'fish tailing' as they went, and this cleared the snow and ice quite effectively.

Reversal at Inchon

At the beginning of September, UN forces were trapped behind the Pusan perimeter, but the KPA was exhausted. The stalemate was broken when the UN launched an amphibious assault at Inchon on the west coast, far behind the front lines. Naturally, the carrier aircraft were heavily involved in this new phase of the war. There were now four carriers in TF-77, though only two – *Valley Forge* and *Philippine Sea* – carried jets. Both had two squadrons of F9Fs.

The landings were to take place on September 15, and for the previous three days the carriers' aircraft

were busy in an effort to soften up and disrupt defences. Air strikes and sweeps occupied all daylight hours. *Valley Forge*'s captain noted that: "jet sorties averaged 36 a day." He explained that "the use of jet aircraft in combat air patrol was extensive. It was found that their obvious advantage of speed over the propeller driven aircraft eliminates the requirement of having the CAP stationed on two or three sides of the force because they can be manoeuvred with as much facility as propeller aircraft and in much less time."

As at Pusan, propeller aircraft took the lion's share of close-support work at first, but in September, *Valley Forge*'s Panthers still undertook 99 offensive sorties, as well as 183 defensive ones.

Later that month, the F9F of Lieutenant Dace from *Philippine Sea* was hit by AA fire near Chorwon, forcing him to eject over the Yellow Sea – the first combat use of an ejection seat. He was in the water for seven hours before the destroyer USS *Chevalier* picked him up.　　　　**»**

BELOW: F2H-2 Banshee # 124968 colliding with a packed forward deck park on USS *Essex*, September 16, 1951, with the loss of seven lives and numerous aircraft. The pilot, Lieutenant (jg) Keller had attempted to land the Banshee after it was damaged in a mid-air collision, it cleared all three barriers and crashed into parked aircraft. US Navy, in the National Archives collection, ref 80-G-433494

Jet vs Jet

The reversal of the situation after the Inchon landings were just as dramatic as the KPA advance in July had been. The KPA, worn out after its drive south and its efforts to break the Pusan perimeter, was now faced with being trapped itself, and began a rapid withdrawal north. In October, South Korea had effectively been liberated and all KPA forces that were able had retreated north of the 38th parallel once again. Rather than accepting the 'status quo ante bellum', the US decided to invade North Korea with the main objective of destroying the KPA, and to reunify the Korean peninsula if possible. Pyongyang was captured on October 19, 1950, and UN forces drove towards the Yalu River on the Chinese border.

The apparent UN victory was shattered in early November when, in response to UN forces' advance, the People's Republic of China (PRC) intervened.

The most significant change that this development brought to the naval aviators of TF77 was that instead of the tiny and mostly ineffectual North Korean Air Force, they would now be facing the Chinese Air Force, a large and modern air arm. Most ominous to the UN was the PRC's MiG-15 swept-wing jet fighters with a performance far in excess of any aircraft they had available, and a heavy armament.

On November 8, the UN forces began a concerted effort to destroy the road and rail bridges across the Yalu. This posed problems for naval aircraft as they had to fly a longer course to the targets so as not to fly over Chinese territory.

While previously TF 77's jets could operate independently of strikes, carrying out sweeps and attacking targets of opportunity, they were now needed to escort the attack aircraft. They typically took off around an hour after the propeller aircraft, rendezvousing close to the target and protecting them for around ten minutes on the approach and for an hour during the attack. A second wave of jets would aim to meet the strike force as it left the target and cover its withdrawal.

A report from USS *Philippine Sea* on November 9 stated: "On this flight, naval aircraft were engaged for the first time by MiG-15 aircraft. One enemy MiG-15 was shot down by the commanding officer, VF-111. This was the first attack by CVG-11 aircraft on the Yalu River bridges."

The report noted: "Defensive tactics used were slight climb at high speed, a left or right fairly steep turn, and a Split-S to enter a dive. The diving characteristics were the best feature of the MiG. The F9F has no trouble countering the tactics mentioned above, except for the high speed dive, which in all cases ended the fight.

The F9F can turn with the MiG and although the MiG appeared faster, the speed advantage is considered to be less than 50 knots."

This would prove to be an optimistic assessment. Indeed, *Valley Forge*'s action report stated: "It is noted with grave concern the reported superior performance of the MiG-15 as compared to the F9F-3. It is believed that if they had been manned by pilots as aggressive and well trained as ours that own pilot and plane losses would have been great." The report suggested "that every means available should be employed in developing a carrier based fighter that will compare favourably" [with the MiG].

On the back foot

The arrival of MiGs changed the situation for the navy's jets. From December, the long range strikes were reduced, and carrier aircraft began to concentrate on targets more easily reachable from the east coast.

The F9F could not stand against well-flown MiG-15s, and defence of strike operations would increasingly shift to the US Air Force's F-86 Sabres. Indeed, USS *Philippine Sea*'s air group went all-prop again in early 1951, with her Panther squadrons replaced with more Corsairs, though the first Marine squadron operating the F9F in Korea, VMF-311, arrived at Yongpo in early December.

ABOVE AND RIGHT: Two USN Douglas F3D-2 Skynight fighters from VC-4 aboard USS *Antietam* in summer 1953 – another detachment of VC-4 was then operating the type in Korea. The Skynight was a large, two-seat aircraft powered by two Westinghouse J34 engines, with a AN/APQ-35 search and targeting radar in the nose for night and poor-weather interceptions. The Skynight did not operate from carriers in the Korean War – aircraft from VC-4 pictured were to operate from USS *Lake Champlain* but caused too much damage to the carrier's deck. Author's collection

The US Navy's evaluation concluded that the interdiction campaign had probably been more costly to the US than to the enemy, when the lost aircraft and men, the resources required to maintain a force of carriers on station, the munitions expended, and the supplies required were measured against the damage done to enemy communications. Steady increases in the volume and effectiveness of North Korean AA gunnery took an ever greater toll on naval squadrons.

The number of jets on each carrier diminished somewhat as the war progressed, with the typical air group of a fleet carrier including one squadron of 18 jets, rather than two squadrons of 12. New types arrived during this phase of the war, with the McDonnell F2H Banshee arriving from August 1951 aboard USS *Essex*. Like the F9F, the Banshee was a straight-winged jet and unable to compete with the MiG-15. It had a similar performance to the Grumman jet, but a longer range, and being twin-engined, had a greater security factor for pilots. The Banshee gained a reputation for toughness and was therefore popular for bridge strikes and rail interdiction. It also had an impressively high ceiling, which enabled its photo-reconnaissance variant to make spy flights over Chinese territory. And the type started to replace the Corsair in the small night-fighter detachments aboard USN carriers.

Another new naval jet type to see service in Korean operations was the Douglas F3D Skynight, which began arriving in theatre in late 1952. This was a specialist two-man all-weather fighter with a large air-interception fire-control radar system. It operated from carriers

only briefly during the Korean War – USS *Lake Champlain* was to have operated Skynights of VC-4 during her deployment in June 1953, but the jets subjected the carrier's wooden deck to too much wear and tear, and after a few patrols, the F3Ds were disembarked to operate from shore bases, from where they became the most successful USN jet of the war in air-to-air combat.

After three years of grinding stalemate, an armistice was signed in July 1953, bringing combat in the Korean War to an end.

Lessons
Carrier jets had performed well during the Korean war but had shown up many of the limitations of operating early generation aircraft from World War Two carriers. Even after the adoption of specially designed carrier jets, the layout, equipment, and size of the typical fleet carrier of the day were inadequate. Added to which the straight-winged jets that were then in service were not competitive against the latest swept-wing jets in use by land-based air forces.

When MiG-15s were encountered over Korea, a crash programme was instituted to develop suitable swept-wing naval jet aircraft, which included the Grumman F9F-6 Cougar, an evolution of the Panther, and the North American FJ-2 Fury, a naval development of the F-86 Sabre. The Cougar missed the war by a month, and the Fury's development was held up by the need for Sabres, though both were cleared for service and variants operated with the USN into the 1960s.

By the armistice, the USN knew that its main challenge was not with aircraft but with carriers. Radically different ways of operating aircraft from carriers were needed.

From the beginning of 1951, the previously mobile front line became rigid. A war characterised by rapid advances and just as rapid reverses was now static, a war of attrition. TF 77's attentions would mostly be turned against Chinese and North Korean communication routes. Bridges and railways would be the chief targets, and this was immortalised in one of the great films of the Korean War; *The Bridges At Toko Ri*, starring William Holden as F9F pilot Lieutenant Harry Brubaker, was made with considerable support from the USN.

GRUMMAN F9F PANTHER

The first carrier jet to see combat, the effective Panther was superseded by swept-wing aircraft

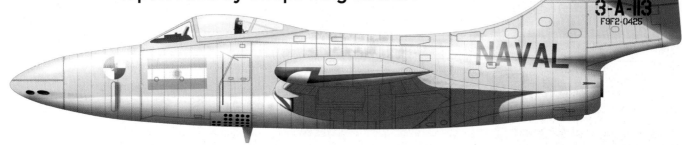

In 1945, Grumman began work on a jet-powered night fighter for the US Navy. The G-75 was to be a large aircraft powered by four Westinghouse 24C-4B engines. Although two prototypes were ordered as the F9F-1, the company concluded it was a dead end.

Instead of backing out, Grumman showed the navy proposals for a single-seat day fighter. Grumman's plans included a twin-engined Westinghouse-powered aircraft or a single-engined machine powered by a Rolls-Royce Nene turbojet buried in the fuselage. The navy rewrote

Grumman's contract and ordered 47 of the Nene-powered fighter as the F9F-2, arranging for Pratt & Whitney to licence-build the Nene as the J42. An alternative version powered by the Allison J33 was designated F9F-3, and in fact more aircraft were ordered to this specification – 54 of them.

The prototype made its first flight on November 21, 1947, and despite

ABOVE: Grumman F9F-2 Panther 3-A-113 of the 1° Escuadrilla Aeronaval de Caza y Ataque (1st Naval Fighter and Attack Squadron), Servicio de Aviacion Naval (Naval Aviation Service), Argentina.
Matthew Willis

ABOVE AND BELOW: F9F-5 Panthers of VF-84 in natural metal on the deck of USS *Antietam* in 1953. While the official colour scheme at the time was Gloss Sea Blue, various problems were experienced with this finish, with high visibility in some conditions and a tendency to erode. From April 1952, a number of aircraft, including F9Fs, had their paint stripped and a protective clear coating applied. Author's collection

PANTHER DATA	
F9F-2	
Length	11.28m (37ft)
Span	11.58m (38ft)
Height	3.73m (12ft 3in)
Empty weight	4,220kg (9,303lb)
Maximum weight	8,842kg (19,494lb)
Maximum speed	925kph (575mph)
Range	2,176km (1,175nm)
Engine	J42-P-8, 5,000lb thrust dry, 5,750lb with water injection
Armament	Four × 20mm M3 cannon 800 rounds, six × 5in HVAR rocket, or six × 250lb bomb, or four × 500lb bomb, or two × 1,000lb bomb
F9F-5	
As F9F-2 unless otherwise specified	
Length	11.83m (38ft 9in)
Empty weight	4,602kg (10,147lb)
Maximum weight	8,492kg (18,721lb)
Maximum speed	972kph (604mph)
Range	2,037km (1,100nm)
Engine	J48-P-6/6A, 6,250lb thrust dry, 8,750lb with afterburner
Total Production all models: 1,382	

the loss of the second prototype to a crash during carrier trials, development proceeded swiftly. The Allison-powered F9F-3 was actually first into service, with VF-51, but the J42-powered -2 proved so superior that most Panthers ordered as -3s were completed with the Pratt & Whitney engine.

The Panther went into combat with VF-51 and VF-52 of USS *Valley Forge* in the Korean War and though its 20mm cannon initially proved troublesome and its low endurance taxed the carriers' deck operation capacity, it proved effective as a daylight 'intruder' in the absence of much opposition in the air.

This changed when MiG-15s began appearing over the battlefield in November 1950. Although the initial engagements between Panthers and MiGs went well for the naval jets, with VF-111's commanding officer shooting one down, the USN was in no doubt that the Panther was outclassed, even when the improved F9F-5 began to arrive. The -5 was powered by a more powerful afterburning J48, and was longer, with a larger tail than the -2.

The first -5s were delivered in late 1950, reaching Korea in October 1952, when it swiftly supplanted the earlier version. US Navy and Marine squadrons operated the Panther in Korea for the duration of the conflict.

A reconnaissance version of both -2 and -5 was produced – the earlier version mostly converted from fighters, but the F9F-5P was purpose-built. It contained cameras in an extended nose and lacked any armament.

By 1954, more than half the USN's fighter squadrons operated the Panther, but after the Korean War the type was progressively withdrawn from frontline use, replaced with swept-wing jets. The last Panthers in service were converted as target drones from the late 1950s, serving until the mid-1960s.

Argentina purchased 24 surplus F9F-2s for the Servicio de Aviacion

LEFT: US Marine Corps F9F-5 Panther #125614 of VMA-223 'Bulldogs'. This squadron converted to the Panther in 1950 and trained many aircrew who flew the type in Korea, though the squadron itself remained in Japan. This aircraft is seen at MCAS Cherry Point after VMA-223's return to the US.
Author's collection

PANTHER TIMELINE

First flight – November 21, 1947	
Entry into service –May 8, 1949	
First carrier deployment – May 1, 1950	
First combat sortie – July 3, 1950	
First air-to-air kill – July 3, 1950 (Yakovlev Yak-9P)	
First jet kill – November 8, 1950 (MiG-15)	
Withdrawn frontline US Navy – 1956	
Withdrawn frontline US Marines – 1957	
Withdrawn training US Navy/Marines – 1958	
First Argentine Panther delivered – August 1958	
Last drone use – c.1965	

PANTHER VARIANTS

F9F-2 – initial service variant, J42 engine, 564 produced	
F9F-2B – fighter-bomber variant, additional bomb carriage	
F9F-2P – photographic reconnaissance variant, converted from -2s	
F9F-3 – alternative with Allison J33, most converted to -2	
F9F-4 – lengthened model with uprated J33, 109 built	
F9F-5 – -4 fuselage with J48 engine, 616 produced	
F9F-5P – photographic reconnaissance variant, 28 produced	

Naval, aircraft arriving from mid-1958. The Argentine navy had an aircraft carrier, ARA *Independencia*, – although the Panthers did not routinely operate from it, as the catapults were deemed not powerful enough. However, deck trials took place in 1963. Panthers

took part in the Argentine Naval Revolt in 1962–1963, strafing army units opposing the mutiny, and along with AT-6 Texans and F4U Corsairs, destroyed a number of tanks. The Panthers last saw combat during a border dispute with Chile in 1965 and were withdrawn in 1969.

BELOW: After the Panther was withdrawn from frontline service, it served for several more years as an advanced trainer. F9F-5 #125949 is seen in USN white and red training colours at Naval Air Station Minneapolis. This aircraft crashed in northeast Minneapolis on May 30, 1957, after colliding with another F9F during a Memorial Day display. Lieutenant (jg) John Forsmark ejected. After several similar incidents, the F9F was withdrawn as a trainer, replaced by Lockheed T-33s
Author's collection

RETHINKING THE CARRIER

The early experience of carrier operations with jet aircraft revealed that there was still much to improve on. Ingenuity, lateral thinking, and science provided the means to turn the carrier jet into a fully practical proposition.

The Korean War presented carrier navies with a dilemma. The experience of the USN with its Essex-class carriers showed that in their current form, little different to how they had fought the last year of World War Two, it was a struggle to operate jets in a combat scenario.

The nature of jet aircraft tended to exacerbate accidents, leading to high operational losses. The frequency of operation put a great deal of strain on equipment, material, and men, just as the increasing weight and speed of jets put strain on flight decks and hardware.

At the same time, the performance of the US Navy's straight-wing jets against the swept-wing MiG-15 demonstrated that the existing technology, marginal as it was for operating from carriers, was not sustainable. Carrier navies needed new aircraft of higher performance and capability to remain competitive, while they also needed to find ways of reducing the strain on carriers and maintaining a high tempo of operations.

Sweeping the skies

By the end of World War Two it was apparent from captured German research that swept wings offered a potentially huge boost in performance. When the first swept-wing fighters appeared in 1947, they were around 100mph or more faster than their straight-winged counterparts. However, they did suffer from poor low-speed control and a tendency to depart suddenly from controlled flight, unacceptable characteristics in a carrier aircraft.

In the late 1940s, Supermarine began to research the problem by modifying its straight-wing naval Attacker jet with a swept wing. The Supermarine Type 510 testbed VV106 was used to make the world's

BELOW: The first swept-wing jet to be approved for the US Navy was the F3H Demon, though it was beaten into service by less ambitious types. The F3H had several developments to enable safe operation of a swept wing, including the drooped leading edge slat and 'all-flying tail' visible here.
Author's collection

first swept-wing jet carrier landings in 1950. It was modified with an arrester hook and two RATOG (rocket assisted take-off gear) units on either side of the fuselage. On November 8, Supermarine test pilot Mike Lithgow and two naval pilots, Lieutenant Commander Doug Parker, and Lieutenant Commander Jock Elliott, each made landings and take-offs on the carrier HMS *Illustrious*. According to Lithgow: "The trial went exceedingly well until the last take-off. For some reason never satisfactorily explained, possibly an 'underproof' RATOG unit, the port wing dropped as Doug Parker became airborne. By the greatest good fortune it struck the flat top of the forward port 4.5in gun turret. This literally threw him back into level flight, from which he was able to accelerate away in the orthodox and accepted manner."

Although it had been touch and go, the Supermarine 510 claimed the important 'first' and proved beyond doubt that swept wing jets could be operated from a carrier. There was a world of difference between a successful trial with highly experienced pilots, however, and routine operations with newly trained aircrew, minimising accidents, and delays.

Various developments to the aircraft carrier and its equipment, outlined below, would mitigate many of the problems of operating swept-wing jets from carriers. In 1950, however, these were in the future. An important focus of work in the meantime would be on the wing itself.

In late 1950, with reports of US Navy pilots over Korea resounding through the corridors of power, the US adopted three approaches simultaneously. The first was to initiate a swept-wing model of an existing jet, which became the F9F-6 Cougar; the second was to order a naval adaptation of a USAF swept-wing jet, leading to the North American FJ-2; the third was to accelerate development of a new medium-range all-weather fighter with the highest possible performance – the McDonnell F3H Demon.

The earliest swept wings had very poor characteristics for deck landing, but designers were already working on improvements. Revised structures, aerofoil sections, high-lift devices, control methods and control surfaces all helped to lower stalling speeds and improve control down to the stall.

This evolution was rapid enough that when the North American FJ-4 was developed, its wing was thinner than that of the previous FJ-3 and offered higher top-end performance, but through developments such as camber, slotted and spoilered flaps, and leading-edge slats, it had better low-speed performance too.

The Demon was the first aircraft designed from the outset with a swept wing for operation from USN carriers. It stemmed from a 1948 request for an interceptor, but Korean experience meant its specifications were modified to broaden its capabilities to an all-weather general purpose fighter, with a search radar and increased fuel capacity. **»**

ABOVE: Supermarine Type 510 VV106, the first swept-wing jet to land on a carrier alighting on HMS *Illustrious* in late 1950. The Type 510 was an interim type based on an Attacker airframe with new swept tail surfaces. It retained the idiosyncratic taildragger layout of its predecessor.
Author's collection

LEFT: Supermarine Type 525 VX138 on its first flight, April 27, 1954, piloted by former naval pilot Mike Lithgow. The 525 was developed into the Supermarine Scimitar, and was fitted with 'Super Circulation,' a form of flap blowing to lower landing speed.
Author's collection

The F3H's wing was swept 40°, more than the MiG-15 and F-86 Sabre but had to have a low stalling speed and positive control down to the stall. It was fitted with powered, connected leading-edge slats and large slotted flaps. Aircraft such as the Demon and Fury were also fitted with extendable nosewheel legs to increase angle of attack for take-off. The British Fleet Air Arm adopted a more basic solution, of fitting a retractable tail bumper on aircraft like the Supermarine Scimitar so it could be launched sitting on its tail, the nosewheel high in the air.

Counter-intuitively, engines of greater power also helped, as they compensated for increases in weight.

Finally

The Fleet Air Arm may have beaten the USN to landing a jet, and a swept wing jet on an aircraft carrier but in all important respects it lagged significantly behind. It was much slower to bring new technologies and aircraft into the front line. The Hawker Sea Hawk first flew in September 1947, three months before the Grumman F9F, which had effectively the same engine and a very similar performance. However, the Sea Hawk did not enter service until March 1953, three and a half years after the F9F joined first line squadrons with the USN, and less than a year before that type would begin to be phased out. UK forces, cash-strapped after the end of World War Two, could not afford the variety of types and the pace of development that the USN, even in peacetime, achieved, and this left the FAA struggling to keep up with the state of the art.

A swept-wing version of the Sea Hawk was trialled but not adopted. The first swept-wing jet to enter service with the FAA was the Supermarine Scimitar in June 1958 – five years after the USN had introduced the Grumman Cougar.

What follows are the top six developments that enabled carriers to operate the latest aircraft:

6: Boundary-layer control

The Scimitar was a large, heavy, and powerful aircraft, with a loaded weight double that of the Sea Hawk and four times the power. In order to ensure control at landing speed, Supermarine incorporated a system they called 'Super Circulation', and which would later become known as boundary-layer control. This was a method of ensuring airflow remained attached to flying surfaces below airspeeds when it would usually break down. High-pressure air was ducted from the jet engines' compressors and blown out of a slot in the trailing edge of the wing. In the Scimitar it was restricted to the wing flaps, while later aircraft used it for the whole wing and tailplanes, but even this reduced landing speed by 12mph. It also had the effect of reducing the angle of attack, which improved the pilot's visibility for landing. The system would go on to be used by many naval jets, as aircraft grew larger and performance higher.

The Scimitar, like its contemporary the de Havilland Sea Vixen all-weather fighter, was hamstrung by the early insistence that it be capable of free (uncatapulted) take-off from a carrier deck. This required a relatively thick wing, which reduced top-end performance. By the time both jets came into service, it was widely accepted that catapult launches would be the norm, but by this time it was far too late to change the design.

Refuelling: "Any pilot who can formate on another aircraft is capable of refuelling his aircraft in the air by the Probe and Drogue method." The pilot had simply to formate on the tanker aircraft and fly his probe into the drogue trailed at the end of the hose. When a connection was made, the fuel would automatically begin to flow, and would cease when the receiving aircraft dropped back. The system of one combat aircraft refuelling another became known as 'buddy-buddy' refuelling.

4: Optical landing system

Between the wars, most carrier navies adopted a human signal operator to guide aircraft onto the deck, constantly informing pilots with 'bats' or 'paddles' whether they were on the correct trajectory and making the final decision as to whether a pilot should complete or abort the landing. Only the Imperial Japanese Navy differed, with a system of lights arranged beside the flight deck.

After the war, the ever greater size and speed of aircraft meant that it was harder and harder for pilots to see and respond to the 'batsman,' or 'paddles,' as the FAA and USN respectively called them. Accident rates were steadily increasing in both navies.

In 1951, RN test pilot Commander Nick Goodhart realised that by careful arrangement of lights and a curved mirror, it should be possible for the pilot of a landing aircraft to see where they were in relation to the ideal trajectory, far further out than they would be able to see the 'batsman'. Moreover, it took subjective judgements and human error out of the equation. The RAE tested his ideas in 1953, constructing an apparatus that showed the pilot ⟩⟩

ABOVE: Hawker Sea Hawk XE435 of 806 'Ace of Diamonds' Squadron crashing into the 'Spider's Web' barrier aboard HMS *Eagle* in the Mediterranean in 1959.
Author's collection

5. Buddy-buddy refuelling

The short range of carrier jet aircraft, and the payload limitations imposed by carrier launching were a particular problem in the 1950s, and for all the improvements made since then, it is a problem that persists. One means of extending range, boosting useful payload, or both used by land-based aircraft was in-flight refuelling – something that was available to North Korean MiG-15bis aircraft but not their USN adversaries. The limitations of space and airframe numbers on carriers mean dedicated tankers would not be possible, but in the 1950s, a means of a carrier air group's existing aircraft refuelling each other was developed.

In-flight refuelling was developed by Alan Cobham in the 1930s, and after World War Two, the Flight Refuelling company he set up developed a system for individual small combat aircraft to become tankers. The Mk 20 refuelling unit was designed to fit on a standard weapons pylon without further modification. It was a self-contained tanker unit, with a drogue and hose, providing its own power and containing its own fuel, although it

RIGHT: FJ-2 Fury flown by Lieutenant Commander C.M. Cruse lines up on the new steam catapult of USS *Hancock* during 'Project Steam', the service trials of the new launcher in July 1954.
Author's collection

could also be fuelled from the aircraft acting as tanker.

This way, a strike could be flown off with a heavy payload that would otherwise severely restrict the quantity of fuel that could be carried, then fuel topped up by another aircraft from the carrier fitted with a refuelling pod. According to Flight

if they were on the correct path, and whether they were high or low of the ideal slope. This worked well at Farnborough, so was transferred to HMS *Illustrious*.

The trials with a DH Sea Vampire were an unqualified success.

As they had with the angled deck, the USN replicated the experiment and came to the same conclusion. The system was known as the Mirror Landing Sight, but when the mirror was replaced with a Fresnel lens, allowing greater information to be imparted to the pilot, this changed to the Optical Landing System (OLS).

Even with the change from mirror to Fresnel lens, the principle is the same, and the OLS remains in use to this day.

3: The 'Spider's Web' crash barrier

The conventional crash barrier used in World War Two consisted of a pair of steel cables stretched athwartships across the deck with thinner cables forming a wide mesh. It worked well at stopping piston-engined aircraft, with a propeller to catch the wires and the engine to absorb the impact. However, the first generation of jets had the cockpit at the extreme nose meaning that if the barrier were too high, it could decapitate the pilot. If it were too low, and the undercarriage failed to snag the wire (or as often happened in practice, it was simply sliced off) the aircraft could ride over it.

The angled deck obviated the main purpose of the crash barrier – protecting aircraft parked forward – but there was still the problem of what to do if an aircraft's arrester hook failed or it was otherwise damaged and could not land in the usual way.

The RAE's Naval Air Department developed a new kind of barrier for use with jets in these scenarios in the early 1950s. Instead of steel, the new barrier used elasticated nylon, and was dubbed the 'Spider's Web'. It could be assembled in around two minutes in the event of a pilot calling an emergency, and when engaged, gently brought a crashing aircraft to a halt without harm to the pilot. As with so many British developments of this period, it was adopted by most other carrier navies.

2: Steam catapult

By the Korean War it was apparent that carrier aircraft had reached the limit of weight and performance that the existing hydraulic catapult could handle. At the same time, the ever greater weight of naval aircraft meant that use of the catapult had gone from an exceptional circumstance to a routine one and would likely be more so in the future.

The idea for the steam catapult had been proposed before World War Two but it wasn't pursued, as developments of the existing catapults driven by hydraulic rams were adequate to carrier navies' immediate needs.

The prospect of naval aircraft of significantly greater size and weight at the end of World War Two prompted the earlier research to be dusted off, aided by launch ramps from German V-1 flying bombs.

The idea was simple – a ram driven along a cylinder by freely available high-pressure steam from the ship's boilers. Two such cylinders were arranged alongside each other beneath the flight deck, with the rams linked by an arm. The shuttle to propel the aircraft was attached to the connecting arm, through a slot in the deck. Finally, a steel bridle was attached to the shuttle and looped onto the aircraft's towing hooks.

The steam catapult had much greater propulsive power than the hydraulic catapult, smoother acceleration, and did away with the hydraulic catapult's need for wire rope tackles that geared the shuttle to an appropriate speed.

LEFT: The first prototype Supermarine Scimitar hooked up to the steam catapult of HMS *Ark Royal* for its carrier trials in 1956. The 'tail down' launch was adopted to help the aircraft attain lift at heavier loads. Author's collection

BELOW: The angled deck of HMS *Ark Royal*, the first carrier to be completed with this vital innovation, is clearly apparent here in this photograph showing de Havilland Sea Vixen prototype XF828 during carrier trials in April 1956. Author's collection

In 1951, a steam catapult was fitted on top of HMS *Perseus'* flight deck, with a dummy deck above it. After its own trials, the RN lent *Perseus* to the USN, which succeeded in putting the catapult into service on its own ships from 1954 beginning with USS *Hancock*, a year before the RN installed its first operational steam catapult on HMS *Ark Royal*.

The steam catapult is still in use on most conventional carriers after 70 years and is only just beginning to be replaced by an electromagnetic catapult.

1: Angled deck

The most significant development that enabled high-performance aircraft to operate routinely from carriers was the angled deck – making the flight deck slightly diagonal to the axis of the ship. This counterintuitive idea solved many problems of carrier aviation at a stroke. It allowed aircraft to be parked on deck and yet also afforded a clear path for aborted landings. It allowed landings and take-offs to take place at the same time. It allowed additional catapults to be installed, increasing the number of aircraft that could be launched. Most importantly, it eliminated the risk of the deck accidents that had blighted operations off Korea, when

barriers had all too often failed to stop crashing jets, allowing them to crash into parked aircraft.

The 'flexible deck' experiments in the late 1940s (see Early Steps) are generally, and accurately, seen as a white elephant, but they did inspire the angled deck, and for that alone they must be regarded as highly valuable. Captain D.R.F. Campbell, the deputy chief naval representative at the Ministry of Supply, was an experienced naval aviator. He had seen some of the proposed layouts for the flexible deck, with the flight deck on one side and parking space next to it. Placing both spaces next to each other would have been impossible on existing carriers, and made new-build carriers far too wide, but there was clearly benefit in separating the space.

The idea itself to cant the flight deck off to one side may have come from experiments at the Royal Aircraft Establishment around the end of World War Two. RAE engineer Geoffrey Cooper was working on developments to carrier design. He recalled: "On one occasion they wanted to put on a special, different-shaped deck on the scale model of the light fleet carrier, so we had it made in the workshop. This was a plank in the shape of a deck to lay on the top of this model

just to see what it was like. Well for some reason, this dummy deck was displaced over to one side, and it was photographed like that. My boss, Boddington, saw that – and he developed the angled deck."

Lewis Boddington was the head of the RAE's Naval Air Department, and he did indeed work with Cambell on the angled deck's development.

The RAE concepts showed the flight deck running off the port side of the deck just forward of the carrier's island. All the space to starboard of the flight deck could safely be used to park aircraft. It removed the need for the increasingly problematic crash barrier and allowed longer-travel arrester gear for the heavier aircraft coming into service.

HMS *Triumph* had an angled axis painted on her existing flight deck in 1952, and trials took place with pilots approaching and flying low over the deck, to test if the idea was feasible. The USN took great interest in these experiments and replicated them with one of their own carriers. They were so successful that the following year, USS *Antietam* had a small sponson built onto her port side, allowing a 10° angled deck to be fitted. Both RN and USN rapidly adopted the angled deck, and it became de rigeur for jet operations.

BELOW: Vought F8U-1 Crusader, #145357 of VF-11 demonstrating the value of the angled deck during a dramatic crash on October 21, 1961. The aircraft landed hard, tearing the arrester hook out. As the aircraft plunged over the side, pilot Lieutenant (jg) Kryway ejected, and was recovered unharmed ten minutes later. Such a crash on an axial-deck carrier would have risked multiple fatalities and many aircraft destroyed.
Author's collection

END OF EMPIRE
1956–1972

At the end of World War Two, the UK was still an imperial power. However, in the 1950s and 60s, the Royal Navy's carriers played a major role as Britain's focus changed from maintaining imperial interests, to ensuring the smooth transition to independence.

By the end of 1945, Britain regained most of the territory it had temporarily lost during the war, and reasserted its dominance over nominally independent countries that were effectively client states. Nevertheless, the war had wrought seismic changes to the British Empire. Many countries clamoured for independence, and the UK's shattered economy made it more difficult than ever to maintain the infrastructure of a global empire.

India's independence movement, which had built throughout the war, led to partition, and the emergence

of four new independent states by the end of the 1940s.

From the late 1940s into the 1950s, a number of other countries gained independence while others saw the withdrawal of British presence. The Royal Navy's aircraft carriers soon became central, first to British attempts to retain global influence, and then to the process of decolonisation through the British sphere.

Suez Crisis

In the UK, the debate over the future of the Empire became ever more urgent as the 1940s gave way

to the 1950s. Two competing visions clashed, on whether decolonisation was the future, or if Britain's place in the world was inextricably bound to the Empire. Winston Churchill's narrow victory in the 1951 election shifted Britain's policy toward the latter. Britain's influence in the Middle and Far East was seen as dependent on its military base in Suez on the Red Sea, and part ownership of the Suez Canal.

Increasing tensions in the region, exacerbated by Egypt's deteriorating relationship with the USA, led to President Gamal Abdul Nasser unilaterally nationalising the

BELOW: Westland Wyvern S4s of 830 Squadron on the flight deck of HMS *Eagle* during preparations for Operation Musketeer in 1956.
Author's collection

Canal in 1956, twelve years before it was supposed to revert to Egyptian control.

Britain's standing in the region was dealt a powerful blow, but international opinion was divided, and the United Nations was unlikely to sanction military action by the UK and France. The US in particular was firmly opposed to a military solution.

With no international backing to take back control of the canal by force, the British and French governments made a clandestine deal with Israel, whose shipping had been barred from the canal and the Gulf of Aqaba by Nasser. Israel was already considering military action against Egypt, and this would provide a pretext for the UK and France to occupy the canal zone militarily, ostensibly to protect the waterway.

The Royal Navy's aircraft carriers would be central to the operation, which was dubbed Operation Musketeer (Opération Mousquetaire in its French elements). There were no fewer than five RN carriers involved in Operation Musketeer, although two were acting as commando carriers. The large fleet carrier *Eagle*, and Centaur-class light fleet carriers *Albion* and *Bulwark* would operate fixed-wing aircraft in the offensive strike role. The older and smaller *Ocean* and

Theseus were allocated as commando carriers, with a secondary function as hospital ships.

In contrast to the FAA's operations in the Korean War just three years earlier, where all its aircraft had been piston-engined, the aircraft complement for Suez operations was almost entirely jet or turbine powered. The only piston-engined types were a handful of radar-equipped Airborne Early Warning (AEW) Skyraiders aboard *Albion* and *Eagle*, and the Sycamore and Whirlwind helicopters aboard *Theseus*.

The main jet type involved would be the Hawker Sea Hawk, a straight-winged fighter-bomber powered by a single Rolls-Royce Nene engine. It was comparable in performance and capability with the USN's Grumman F9F Panther, and was now available in its definitive FGA6 form, capable of carrying bombs and rockets. During Operation Musketeer, Sea Hawks were operated by 800 and 802 Squadrons aboard *Albion*, 897 and 898 Squadrons aboard *Eagle*, and 804, 810 and 895 Squadrons aboard *Bulwark*.

The other pure jet type to see action at Suez was the de Havilland Sea Venom all-weather fighter. This was operated by 809 Squadron aboard *Albion*, and 892 and 893 Squadrons aboard HMS *Eagle*, the latter replacing a squadron of Fairey Gannet anti-submarine aircraft. Also aboard HMS *Eagle* were the Westland Wyvern turboprop-powered strike fighters of 830 Squadron.

Two French light fleet carriers, *Arromanches* and *La Fayette*, were involved too but they both operated a propeller type only, the Vought F4U Corsair.

In the expectation of military action, the ships and units of the taskforce prepared as thoroughly as possible for the task ahead.

Operation Musketeer

In late October 1956, Israeli tanks began a thrust into the Sinai peninsula, quickly overcoming Egyptian forces. On October 30, the UK and French governments issued an ultimatum to Israel and Egypt to stop the fighting, or they would launch military action. When, predictably, the ultimatum was ignored, Operation Musketeer was initiated.

On November 1, FAA carrier aircraft commenced an intensive series of attacks against Egyptian targets, in conjunction with RAF and French aircraft. Sea Hawks and Sea Venoms, though the latter were principally night-fighters, flew off *Albion, Bulwark* and *Eagle* to attack airfields with rockets and cannon. Meanwhile, Wyverns of 830 Squadron each carried a 1,000lb bomb in 'runway denial' attacks – the first aircraft in to attack the former British air station at Dekheila was the squadron's commanding officer, Lieutenant Commander Howard, whose bomb went plum into the intersection of two runways and the resulting crater put both out of use, although after the raid it was judged that one of the three runways remained useable. On this operation, Sea Hawks of 897 and 899 Squadrons provided a Combat Air Patrol (CAP) over the attacking Wyverns.

The priority was to knock out the Egyptian Air Force (EAF) MiG-15s, which were just as superior to the FAA's aircraft as they had been to the USN's straight-wing jets over »

ABOVE: Westland Wyvern S4 WL888 of 830 Squadron firing a salvo of rocket projectiles during armament training in the run-up to Operation Musketeer. Rockets were a much-used weapon by the FAA during Musketeer, but Wyverns generally used 1,000lb bombs.
Author's collection

Korea, before they could get into the air. The concerted FAA strikes in the morning destroyed an estimated 58 aircraft on the ground at three airfields, with the total at the end of the day for the naval aircraft standing at around 80.

The EAF had been overwhelmingly focussed on countering the Israeli incursion into Sinai to the east and was not at all prepared to respond to British and French air attacks from the north. It was clear that the EAF was not in a position to oppose the FAA in the air, so the carrier air groups were able to direct their attentions almost exclusively against ground targets. *Eagle*'s two Sea Venom squadrons joined the operation the following day, with an attack on Almaza airfield, while 830 returned to Dekheila.

Flak, however, was the biggest threat. On the first day it had generally been light and ill-aimed, but by the second it was to be feared and respected. A hit to Lieutenant Commander Wilcox's Sea Venom wrecked the hydraulic system, and wounded the Observer, Flight Officer Olding, who would lose his leg as a result of the injuries. Wilcox made a successful wheels-up landing on *Eagle*, but it proved that even without much opposition in the air, operations over Egypt could be dangerous.

The following day, the main effort was directed at communications. The Wyverns dive-bombed a bridge over the Nile, leaving it standing but dangerously undermined. Lieutenant McCarthy's aircraft was hit by the ever more dangerous flak, and he was forced to eject three miles offshore. Undeterred, the squadron returned later in the morning and finished knocking the bridge down.

On November 4, FAA operations switched to targets that would assist the imminent landings by British and French ground troops, such as coastal defences and AA batteries. Nevertheless, that morning Sea Hawks and Sea Venoms from *Albion* hit Cairo International Airport again, and some of the fighters were diverted against three fast attack boats that harassing naval forces off the Nile Delta. The jets sank two and damaged the third, but as it was no longer a threat, the aircraft allowed the remaining boat to pick up survivors from the other two and withdraw.

Paratroopers landed on November 5, and the FAA aircraft were detailed to support them. A 'cab rank' system was set up with rocket-armed Sea Hawks and Sea Venoms called onto specific targets by controllers on the ground.

The following day, under huge international pressure, a ceasefire began, though FAA aircraft continued to fly CAP and armed reconnaissance sorties over the occupied areas as an attempted show of strength.

For HMS *Eagle*, the voyage home took on a tragic cast.

An inadvertently fired gun in the hangar caused a fire, which killed an 830 Squadron maintainer.

Aftermath

The Suez Crisis of 1956 had a profound and lasting effect on the UK, which would affect the path of British naval aviation over the coming decades. The political fallout made Britain's loss of prestige and trust permanent and paved the way for a smaller role in the world. This would not become apparent for many years, but much of the future shape of British carrier aviation can be traced back to the disastrous adventure in Egypt.

The FAA had performed well at Suez, though it had been helped by the EAF's disarray, and many of its more modern aircraft being moved to safety in neighbouring countries when the scale of the threat was apparent. A good sortie rate had been achieved, good serviceability in the aircraft, and the strikes had been effective despite strong anti-aircraft gunfire.

After the political disaster of Suez, the RN's carriers would be kept busy, their aircraft and their mere presence often called for amid the postwar atmosphere of decolonisation. From then on, however, they would generally find themselves operating on the side of international opinion and in support of the self-determination of people in countries emerging from colonialism.

One such activity was Operation Vantage in 1961, aimed at deterring Iraq from invading the newly independent state of Kuwait.

Under the terms of the end of the British 'protectorate' of Kuwait, the country had the right to ask the UK for military assistance. Belligerent rhetoric from Abdul Karim Qassim, who had seized power in Iraq three years earlier, led to assistance being requested on June 30, 1961.

The carrier HMS *Victorious*, with its Supermarine Scimitar and new DH Sea Vixen jets, was among the first naval forces to be dispatched, providing air defence for commandos going ashore.

The conditions were tricky, with light winds and shallow waters inshore, but when a suitable operating area was established, the carrier quickly got into a routine of four days flying and two days' rest and replenishment. Serviceability of aircraft was poor at first, but this improved, and the Sea Vixen, according to the commander-in-chief of Operation Vantage, "Provided for the first time a reasonably sophisticated day and night air defence for the forces in Kuwait." »

ABOVE: ...And suffering a pulled-out arrester hook, followed by a left main undercarriage collapse. The brakes could not stop the Sea Hawk by itself, and it crashed into WM985 before falling over the side. The pilot, Sub Lieutenant Waddington, survived and was rescued by helicopter.
Author's collection

that: "The presence of *Ark Royal* in the Far East during the height of the Indonesian confrontation of Malaysia was undoubtedly not only a stabilising but a restraining influence."

The flag officer, Middle East pointed out that the RAF had been unable to provide air defence to the forces ashore, but the RN had stepped into the breach quite effectively, with a combination of an air-defence frigate stationed inshore and the carrier offshore.

The Scimitars, meanwhile, were a useful supplement to the RAF's Hunters in the ground attack role, although lack of wind meant they had to be launched without long-range tanks and thus could spend only 12 minutes over the operational area. *Victorious* was relieved by *Centaur* in July, and the Arab League took over defence in October. Qassim was persuaded not to invade, though the situation remained tense and the UK kept forces available to support Kuwait for a decade.

A similar confrontation between Indonesia and Malaysia in 1964 saw several Royal Navy carriers showing the flag and demonstrating Britain's preparedness to step in. HMS *Ark Royal*'s commander, Captain M.F. Fell, wrote to the ship's company

As a demonstration of capabilities, the major exercise 'Guardrail' was carried out in August 1965. This included live weapon training on the USN practice ranges at the Subic Bay base, in which 803 Squadron sharpened up its abilities with the Bullpup air-to-surface missile. The Airborne Early Warning (AEW) Gannets of 849C Squadron located USS *Midway* during night exercises, then controlled *Ark Royal*'s fighters in air-to-air engagements. Only 890 Squadron's Sea Vixen FAW 1 crews were left somewhat frustrated, as the squadron's programme with Firestreak air-to-air missiles was hampered by unserviceable towed targets. Of 12 planned firings, only three went ahead.

Finally, in the third phase of Exercise Guardrail, low-level strikes were made against targets on the coast of Borneo, and exercises carried out with Forward Air Controllers on the ground. These mostly went off smoothly, apart from Lieutenant Rankin of 803 Squadron suffering the first barrier crash of the commission with his Scimitar. On September 4, *Ark Royal* returned to Singapore.

RIGHT: Supermarine Scimitars of 803 Squadron and DH Sea Vixens of 892 Squadron aboard HMS *Victorious* at around the time of Operation Vantage, to deter Iraq from invading Kuwait.
Author's collection

The Battle of Beira

In the 1960s, with the decolonisation movement in full flow across the British Empire, the British government adopted a policy known as 'No independence before majority rule', (NIBMAR). In other words, no country could leave the British Empire if it had not handed control to the majority population. This was strongly opposed by the white minority governors of Rhodesia in southern Africa, leading to Prime Minister Ian Smith unilaterally declaring independence in November 1965.

Just as with Britain in Suez 11 years earlier, the international community was firmly against Rhodesia's actions, and sanctions were swiftly imposed. This time, Britain was on the side of international opinion and the progress of decolonisation. In fact, with no small irony, the UN backed military action, which Britain was unwilling to take without severe provocation.

Instead, the government authorised the military to take steps to back up sanctions. This included Royal Navy carriers being sent to the region to discourage breaches of the international sanctions. Most notably, Rhodesia could be supplied with oil by tankers via Beira in Mozambique, then a Portuguese colony, as a pipeline had been laid to Salisbury (now Harare). A

naval patrol was proposed to establish the nationality of any tanker putting into Beira, to ensure that countries that supported the sanctions were not themselves in breach.

First on station was HMS *Ark Royal*, which was then temporarily operating from Mombasa in order to relieve HMS *Eagle*. The 'Beira Patrol' was backed with a UN resolution, although it soon became clear that apartheid South Africa and colonialist Portugal were keen to support the rogue state, and the sanctions initially did not have the desired effect. Although the subsequent military operation did not involve combat, it was dubbed 'The Battle of Beira' by *Ark Royal*'s personnel. **»**

ABOVE: HMS *Ark Royal* arriving in Freemantle, Australia, with the Supermarine Scimitar day fighters of 800 Squadron ranged forward, the DH Sea Vixens of 890 Squadron and Fairey Gannets of 831/849 Squadron amidships, and Westland Wessex helicopters of 815 Squadron astern. *Ark Royal* was often to be found 'east of Suez' in the 1960s.
Author's collection

LEFT: Scimitar XD280 of 800 Squadron about to launch from *Ark Royal* in 1962. This aircraft was one of those used by the squadron to patrol the Aden colony's border with Yemen during a period of unrest that year.
Author's collection

Ark Royal arrived in the Mozambique Channel in March 1966.

Here, the Gannets of 849C Squadron really came into their own. The turboprop AEW aircraft used their old but capable AN/APS-20 radar sets to provide 24-hour surveillance over the entire Mozambique Channel. Ark Royal's commission book added that: "These could, however, profit by assistance from the swifter Sea Vixen and Scimitar aircraft which could rapidly swoop down and identify or photograph the more distant contacts on the Gannet radar." Helicopters could inspect vessels that passed close enough to Ark.

To the amusement of all in the AEW flight, it was a Gannet that carried out the only air-to-air interception of the deployment when it contacted and headed off a Portuguese 'snooper'. For the fast jets, flying visual probes became somewhat repetitious, and according to the commission book: "The wind and sea conditions of the Mozambique Channel in March and May made getting off the deck more tricky than usual, but, once airborne, we played a valuable role."

Ark Royal's aircraft maintained this tempo for ten days until Eagle returned. Over a period of five years prior to the current commission, Eagle had been fully modernised and was now in a more modern state than Ark Royal, with a fully angled deck, with two new steam catapults at the waist position capable of launching the latest (and heaviest) aircraft, and other improvements such as a superior Type 984 radar. Her air group consisted of AEW Gannets, Sea Vixen all-weather strike fighters in the latest FAW2 variant, and Blackburn Buccaneer S1 strike aircraft. There was also a small contingent of Scimitars to act solely in the refuelling role for the Buccaneers, which, while highly capable, were somewhat underpowered in their S1 version.

Two tankers were spotted by Gannets and identified during this period, including one from a country that supported the blockade, but the procedure for apprehending them had not yet been agreed. Afterwards, a UN resolution would allow the RN to stop vessels with force if necessary. The weather was often bad, but the 24-hour surveillance had to be kept up, which meant launching and recovering aircraft despite Eagle pitching and rolling, and a permanently slippery deck. The carrier remained on station, replenished at sea, for 71 days – a record that stood until the first Gulf War in 1991. Ark Royal returned to relieve Eagle on May 5, 1966, and patrolled until the 25th. By this time, RN frigates had arrived to support the carriers, and the FAA air groups were supplemented by a squadron of RAF Avro Shackleton patrol aircraft. The Beira Patrol was maintained until 1975, and the ongoing trade embargo made Ian Smith agree to majority rule in 1978. The country finally achieved internationally recognised independence as Zimbabwe in 1980.

Drawdown

Enthusiasm over the FAA's successful operations during the Beira Patrol in 1966 were tempered by the government's decision to withdraw from carrier operations when the current fleet was retired. The government, in the midst of a financial slump, considered it most important to focus on NATO commitments in Europe. Carriers, associated with the maintenance of Empire 'east of Suez' no longer seemed as relevant – ironic, given how busy they had been in recent years.

The replacement carriers were cancelled, meaning that the existing three large carriers, Ark Royal, Eagle, and Victorious – all of World War Two origin – would be the last in RN service, unless a future change of policy resurrected the idea. No more than a year after the policy was announced, Victorious was unexpectedly decommissioned, having only just gone through a refit. Ark Royal went into the dockyard in 1967 for a planned refit to enable her to operate the FAA's new McDonnell Douglas Phantoms. Eagle would have undergone the same process but for the drawdown of the RN carrier force, with the result that despite being in much better condition than Ark Royal,

with more modern equipment, she was decommissioned in 1972. The Sea Vixen was retired along with *Eagle*, despite many FAW2 airframes having plenty of life left.

Hermes was retained as a commando carrier, and from 1972 *Ark Royal* was the conventional aircraft carrier in British service.

British Honduras

Despite the feeling in government that there was insufficient need for carriers to justify their cost – not to mention that of their air groups – new jobs for the carriers, which only they could fulfil, kept arising. The latest of these took place across the Atlantic in Central America, at the start of 1972. The personnel of *Ark*'s Buccaneer squadron would refer to this, with tongue firmly in cheek, as 'the year 809 saved the Empire, well almost'. A military buildup on the border of neighbouring Guatemala convinced the tiny Crown Colony of British Honduras that an invasion was imminent.

British Honduras was on a slow track to independence. It was the last British territory in the mainland Americas and had become self-governing in 1964. Guatemala had periodically threatened to invade since 1948, and while talks had taken place on several occasions, these had generally failed to reach any kind of settlement. The British government was adamant that the people of British Honduras should get to determine their own future.

Ark Royal had been en route for Norfolk, Virginia but was diverted south at best possible speed. The ageing carrier raced across the Atlantic, ignoring the rough weather which tore radio aerials away and

left the hull looking battered and salt-stained. Potentially, every minute counted. Finally, by January 29, 1972, the carrier was just within range for its Buccaneers to speed to British Honduras and make a very public overflight, warning the Guatemalan government that a British strike carrier was on the way and meant business. Fortunately, the day dawned clear and bright.

Every possible drop of fuel was loaded onto two Buccaneer S2s, with the fitting of internal bomb-bay and underwing slipper tanks. Even so, in-flight refuelling from other Buccaneers (the Scimitar tankers had been retired in August 1966) would be necessary on the way out and the way back.

The squadron commander, Lieutenant Commander Davis, and senior pilot, Lieutenant Commander Walkinshaw, would pilot the two Buccaneers on the extremely long and arduous flight. After hours in

the air, the Yucatan peninsula was sighted, and the two aircraft began to descend. They had fuel for two low-level orbits of Belize City before it was time to head back to *Ark Royal*.

The demonstration did the trick, and Guatemala backed away from an invasion. The colony changed its name to Belize the following year and gained full independence in 1981.

While the RN's conventional fleet carriers did indeed come to an end in 1978 with *Ark Royal*'s final decommissioning, it turned out not to be the end for RN carrier aviation. The development of workable vertical take-off and landing (VTOL) aircraft and small 'command ships' with flight decks kept the door open for RN carrier aviation to continue. And ten years after the British Honduras incident, these ships and aircraft would see the Royal Navy protecting the self-determination of a small dependency across the Atlantic.

ABOVE: Sea Vixen FAW1 XJ521 of 890 Squadron landing on *Ark Royal* in 1961–62. Author's collection

BELOW: Sea Vixen FAW2, distinguished by the extensions to the wing booms forward of the wings, launching from the new, more powerful waist catapult of HMS *Eagle* following her modernisation in 1965. Soon after commissioning, *Eagle* and her aircraft took part in the Beira Patrol off Mozambique. Author's collection

BLACKBURN BUCCANEER

With an advanced low-level strike aircraft, Blackburn Aircraft created one of the outstanding naval types of the jet era.

RIGHT: Buccaneer S2 XV359 '034' of 809 Squadron during a Mediterranean cruise aboard HMS *Ark Royal* in November 1977. Customarily the aircraft 034 and 035 were fitted as aerial tankers with 'buddy' pods.
Matthew Willis

RIGHT: The first pre-production Buccaneer XK523 during carrier trials on HMS *Ark Royal* off Malta in November–December 1960. The folding nose necessary to fit the aircraft into carrier lifts is apparent, as are the tail cone air brakes, which open fully to reduce the aircraft's length.
Author's collection

BELOW: The fifth pre-production Buccaneer XK527 during catapult trials on HMS *Victorious* in the English Channel in January 1960.
Author's collection

From the end of World War Two, torpedo attack – the chief weapon of most naval air arms – was increasingly difficult to achieve and survive, thanks to radar-laid anti-aircraft guns and guided missiles. A new method of killing enemy warships was needed. The spectacular answer was a tactical nuclear bomb. Pinpoint accuracy was unnecessary: a strike aircraft could race in at low level beneath radar coverage, 'toss' its bomb, and escape in the same manner it arrived. In 1952, the Admiralty submitted requirement NA39 for a carrier-based strike aircraft that could carry a nuclear weapon in an internal bay, flying at Mach 0.85 at 200ft.

As the Cold War set in, it was clear the Soviet Union had ambitions for a blue water navy including powerful heavy cruisers acting as commerce raiders. It is something of a myth that the Buccaneer was created specifically to counter these Sverdlov-class cruisers, but they were an important factor in Admiralty thinking.

Requirement NA39 set out tough performance stipulations, while the aircraft had to be able to operate from small British carriers, with folding wings, and even folding nose and tail to ensure they could fit.

Central to Blackburn's successful entry was Boundary Layer Control (see Rethinking the Carrier), in which high pressure air from the engines was squirted over the flying surfaces to reduce landing speeds and improve control. This was already used on the Supermarine Scimitar's flaps, but on the Blackburn NA39, it would be used over the entire wing and the tailplane. An innovative revolving bomb bay contained the specified nuclear bomb, or 4,000lb of conventional bombs.

Blackburn's airframe would also be immensely strong, with large sections machined from solid metal. It also incorporated the new technique of 'area ruling' to reduce the buildup of shockwaves at high subsonic speeds, by 'waisting' the fuselage where the wing joined. This led to a distinctive bulge aft of the trailing edge. The Buccaneer would be fitted with search radar and an early form of head-up display, together with other advanced features such as moving map display.

Buccaneer appears

The first prototype, XK486, took to the air on April 30, 1958, powered by two de Havilland Gyron Junior engines. Twenty pre-production aircraft helped speed up the development programme immensely, during which the aircraft received the name Buccaneer. In May 1959 'touch-and-go' landings were tried on HMS *Victorious*, then fuller carrier trials took place in 1960 on *Centaur* and *Ark Royal*. The Royal Navy

BUCCANEER DATA

S1

Length	19.33m (63ft 5in)
Span	12.9m (42ft 4in)
Height	4.94m (16ft 3in)
Empty weight	13,520kg (29,800lb)
Maximum weight	28,000kg (45,000lb)
Maximum speed	645mph
Range	2,800km (1,730 miles)
Engine	Two × de Havilland Gyron Junior 101, 3,220kg (7,100lb) thrust
Armament	Up to 8,000lb including 'Red Beard' 2,000lb nuclear bomb, WE.177 1,010lb nuclear bomb, Mk10 1,000lb or Mk21 500lb conventional bomb, 2in rocket pod (each carrying 36 rockets), ventral reconnaissance pack.

S2

As S1 unless otherwise specified	
Span	13.4m (44ft)
Empty weight	14,060kg (31,000lb)
Maximum weight	20,400kg (62,000lb)
Maximum speed	645mph
Range	3,700km (2,300 miles)
Engine	Two × Rolls-Royce Spey 101, 5,125kg (11,300lb) thrust
Armament	Up to 16,000lb, as S1 plus Bullpup, Martel air–surface missiles (Sea Eagle not used on RN Buccaneers)

BUCCANEER TIMELINE

First flight – April 30, 1958

Entry into service – May 1962

First carrier deployment – February 19, 1963

Introduction of S2 –April 9, 1965

Last carrier squadron, 809, formed – January 27, 1966

First operational sortie, Mozambique Channel – 15 March 1966

Last FAA Buccaneer delivered – May 1969

Last carrier deployment, HMS Ark Royal –April 6, 1978

Withdrawal from FAA – December 15, 1978

more powerful and economical Rolls-Royce Spey turbofans. *Ark Royal* carried out clearance trials in March 1964. To enable take-offs at high all-up weights without having to burn off fuel before landing, the test Buccaneer simply took off with a load of inert 1,000lb bombs, which it jettisoned in the sea "to the anguish of the Air Gunner." During these trials, *Ark Royal* became the first RN carrier to launch an aircraft with an AUW of 50,000lb, demonstrating the S2's much increased lifting power.

The final RN carrier to operate the Buccaneer was HMS *Hermes*, when 809 Squadron embarked in 1967, covering the British withdrawal from Aden.

In 1970, Buccaneers rejoined *Ark Royal*, with 809's S2s, proving a capable and flexible part of the carrier's armoury from 1972 to 1978, when it was the only conventional carrier in RN service. This included demonstration flights over British Honduras, dissuading Guatemala from invading (see End of Empire).

The Buccaneer was tough, effective, and high-performing and, particularly with the S2, the equal of any naval strike aircraft anywhere. From 1972, it carried the Martel anti-ship missile, and was capable in ground attack roles as well as maritime strike. It only saw combat with the RAF, after the RN's conventional carriers were retired, but its performance in the First Gulf War proved what an excellent design it was.

ABOVE: Buccaneers at low level – closest, XK526, the first S2, demonstrating the much wider air intakes for the Spey engines that distinguish this mark. Behind, S1 XN953. Author's collection

BELOW: Early production Buccaneer S1 XN934 of 801 Squadron landing aboard HMS *Ark Royal* in 1962, during the type's first carrier embarkation. The aircraft wears all-over anti-flash white, reflecting its early nuclear role. Author's collection

ordered 40 aircraft of the S1 variant in 1959, and these began to arrive in 1962, with further orders following.

Ark Royal recommissioned in February 1963, with 801 Squadron's Buccaneers for two NATO exercises, before transferring to HMS *Victorious*.

HMS *Eagle* took on 800 Squadron's Buccaneers in 1964, with the type's first operational sorties flown during the 'Beira Patrol' blockade of Rhodesia in 1966 (see End of Empire).

Even before the S1 entered service, the improved S2 was planned, with

COLD WAR CONFRONTATION

NATO never went directly to war with the Soviet Union but throughout the Cold War of 1947 to 1991, both maintained a wary watch on each other's activities. A state of military confrontation existed between the powers, and nowhere was that confrontation more apparent than in the skies above naval operations and exercises.

ABOVE: A Vought F-8 Crusader fighter of VF-62 'waves off' USS *Shangri La* during NATO Exercise 'Sword Thrust' in October 1960, part of that year's autumn exercises – the largest in three years, as the Cold War gathered pace. Two members of the Landing Signal Officer's detail watch the jet going around while the man in the foreground stays fixed on the next aircraft in the landing pattern.
Author's collection

By the time jets were common aboard aircraft carriers, the emergent Cold War was dominating military thinking to East and West. The carriers of North Atlantic Treaty Organisation (NATO) navies, such as the US Navy, British Royal Navy, and French Marine Nationale, often found themselves confronting Soviet aircraft and ships, in numerous tense stand-offs across the world's seas. Only a handful of such occasions led to fire being exchanged, and these never led to war, but for nearly 40 years, both sides acted as though war was imminent, and equipped, trained, and prepared for it.

While the actual wars fought throughout that period were often proxy conflicts for the Cold War protagonists, both sides were ultimately focussed on the possibility of a direct military confrontation in Europe, as well as the skies above and the seas around it. NATO carried out frequent, large-scale naval exercises throughout the Cold War period, both to prepare for war with its equivalent, the Warsaw Pact alliance, and to demonstrate the capability and willingness to fight. NATO and Warsaw Pact forces eyed each other warily during naval exercises and routine activities.

An indication that the USSR intended to transform its small, locally focussed navy into a major ocean-going force was illustrated by the instigation of the Sverdlov-class cruiser, the first of which was launched in 1950. Some 25–30 of these

were originally planned, which would have represented a major threat to Atlantic convoys. In particular, their powerful anti-aircraft armament was a worry for carrier-based aircraft of the early 1950s.

Battle-cruisers and aircraft carriers were planned too, representing a serious statement of intent. Though only 14 Sverdlovs were completed in the end, and the larger warships cancelled altogether, the Soviet Navy was still transformed into a force with global reach and influence.

Though the Soviet Navy did not introduce aircraft carrying ships until the late 1960s, with no fixed-wing carrier capability until the mid-1970s, it built up a strong land-based air arm which proved a constant headache to NATO.

In particular, the Tupolev Tu-16 (NATO reporting name *Badger*) jet bomber, which was approved for production in July 1952 and entered service less than two years later, was a capable long-range maritime reconnaissance bomber, able to carry radar-guided anti-ship missiles from the outset. Equally, the performance of the Tu-16's reconnaissance variants meant it was hard not to give away valuable information about NATO navies every time they put to sea.

Later, the Tu-95 *Bear* long range strategic bomber was adapted to the maritime reconnaissance role too, while other types such as the Ilyushin Il-20M *Coot* furnished electronic intelligence (ELINT) and communications intelligence (COMINT) for the Soviet Navy. Intercepting these aircraft and shepherding them away from NATO exercises, operations and routine activities at sea became a common role for carrier aircraft in the Cold War era.

A further threat was the buildup of long-range submarines, beginning with the Project 613 and associated developments (NATO reporting name *Whiskey*), of which over 200 were built in the 1950s. With nuclear attack submarines arriving from the late 1950s, NATO carriers needed a sophisticated anti-submarine capability.

In the years immediately following World War Two, Western navies

carried out numerous large exercises in the Norwegian Sea and Greenland Sea. This area had been strategically important since World War One but gained further significance with the rise of the USSR as the chief adversary to US-aligned countries. Those waters played host to the first major combined exercise by NATO navies, Operation Mainbrace of 1952, which involved no fewer than ten aircraft carriers – six from the US Navy (USN), three from the Royal Navy (RN) and one from the Royal Canadian Navy (RCN). The premise of Mainbrace was to simulate the

defence of Norway and Denmark against a Soviet invasion. A similarly large-scale exercise took place five years later with 'Strikeback', testing the response to an all-out nuclear attack by the USSR on NATO. Carrier-based air strikes were a major element of Strikeback, which included nine carriers.

Although these exercises nominally took place in peacetime, they were carried out in deadly earnest and involved plenty of risks. Strikeback took place in poor weather and saw several aircraft lost, including the dramatic end to a Douglas **»**

ABOVE: Fairey Gannet AS.1 trains in anti-submarine warfare with a Royal Navy frigate off the UK coast in the mid-1950s, its ventral 'dustbin' for the search radar extended. Previously, anti-submarine warfare had been conducted by strike aircraft with minimal adaptations, but the increasing sophistication of submarine countermeasures and sensors resulted in specialised aircraft like the turboprop-powered Gannet.
Author's collection

LEFT: The crowded flight deck of USS *Enterprise*, shortly after standing down from duties in the Cuban Missile Crisis. The Douglas A-4 Skyhawk jets of VA-66 and VA-64 along the flight deck edge would have been the primary weapon had *Enterprise* been called upon to support amphibious landings. The A-1 Skyraider and Grumman E-1 Tracer aircraft demonstrate that propeller aircraft still maintained a role well into the jet age.
Author's collection

A-3 Skywarrior, which suffered a ramp strike upon landing on USS *Forrestal*, bursting into flame and plunging into the sea, with the loss of three crewmembers. A Fairey Gannet awaiting take-off from HMS *Eagle* was caught in the propwash of another aircraft and slid over the side, with the loss of two of the three crew. Several other aircraft were also lost, and the total number of deaths reached 11.

Cuban Missile Crisis

In 1962, the Cold War came closer to all-out conflict than at any other time in its four-decade span. Starting in May that year, the USSR's premier Nikita Khrushchev prepared to base R-12 and R-14 missiles with nuclear warheads on the Caribbean island of Cuba, in response to US deployment of nuclear missiles in Italy and Turkey. The deployment would have put large parts of the US in range of nuclear strike, as the Turkish-based missiles did with the USSR.

Cuba had already been the focus of USN carrier deployments during the disastrous US-backed attempt to overthrow Fidel Castro's government in 1961. Task Group Alpha contained the carrier USS *Essex*, distantly supporting the amphibious invasion force, though in the end the invasion was quickly repulsed and the USN did not intervene.

LEFT: Vought RF-8A Crusader reconnaissance fighter of VFP-62 as it appeared during the Cuban Missile Crisis, with photographic technicians loading film into the cameras while the pilot climbs into the cockpit for another mission. Author's collection

BELOW: As well as providing vital reconnaissance of Cuban missile sites in Autumn 1962, VFP-62 provided detachments to several aircraft carriers. Here RF-8A #146864 is seen flying from USS *Shangri La* in 1964, demonstrating the squadron's 'film strip' markings on the wingtips and tail. The modified ventral bay with its camera windows can be seen clearly. Author's collection

The so-called 'Bay of Pigs' episode pushed Castro closer to the USSR, smoothing the way for missile deployments.

Reconnaissance photographs from US Air Force Lockheed U-2s, processed and assessed by USN specialists, had aroused suspicions in Washington but their ultra-high altitude reconnaissance had not provided conclusive proof. To do so would be up to the US Navy, and Operation Blue Moon.

On October 13, two squadrons operating the RF-8A, an adaptation of the Vought F-8 Crusader fighter, were dispatched to Naval Air Station (NAS) Cecil Field in Florida and ordered to stand by. The USN sent the light photographic squadron VFP-62. However, this unit was being pulled in several different directions as it was also required to provide photographic reconnaissance detachments to aircraft carriers in the Pacific Fleet, which were on high alert and ready to go onto a combat footing. To supplement the US Navy squadron, the US Marine unit VMCJ-2 was also brought in, providing Marine pilots and maintenance crews to support VFP-62, while a two-aircraft detachment operated by the squadron itself would fly additional sorties.

The navy Crusaders moved to a forward base at NAS Key West, 100

miles from the coast of Cuba to refuel, with aircraft only returning to Cecil Field for maintenance. From Key West, pairs of aircraft on four hours' notice would take off and streak in at speed, beneath Cuban radar, hoping to avoid the attentions of the surface-air missiles being installed to protect the ballistic missile sites. As they passed over the suspected missile sites, they took

low-level photographs and flew on to NAS Jacksonville, where VFP-62's on-site photographic laboratory allowed the images to be developed immediately. Their operation complete, the RF-8As returned to Cecil Field for maintenance checks, then staged to Key West again for the next operation. The Marine detachment of VMCJ-2, meanwhile operated from Cuba itself, at the naval base at Guantánamo Bay, and undertook high-altitude and night missions.

The first operational Blue Moon flights were made on October 23, with a flight over San Cristóbal, followed by two more flights that day. This increased to ten flights two days later, and 14 flights two days after that. From then on, between two and six flights were flown every day or two until 15 November. The first day's photographs were insufficiently clear, as the RF-8As' approach altitude of 200ft was so low that sea salt coated the camera windows. Afterwards, the approach was flown at a considerably more dangerous 1,000ft until the photographs were safely committed to film, and the Crusaders could drop to low level to escape.

Blue Moon proved beyond doubt that preparations for ballistic missile launch sites were underway.

Becoming fully operational just in time to play a major role in the crisis was the world's first nuclear-powered supercarrier, USS Enterprise (CVAN-65). The carrier left Norfolk in such a hurry that half its air wing was not yet aboard, and a cover story had to be concocted for the speed of the departure.

US forces were by now preparing for air strikes on Cuba, or even »

ABOVE: A de Havilland Sea Vixen FAW2 of 899 Squadron, HMS *Eagle*, shepherds a Tupolev Tu-16 during NATO Exercise Silver Tower in the Norwegian Sea on September 24, 1968. The Tu-16 is a K-10 maritime reconnaissance model with radar in the nose and anti-ship missile capability. Tu-16s were a threat to NATO carriers for most of the Cold War.
Author's collection

a full-scale invasion. *Enterprise* disembarked her squadron of North American A-5 Vigilante nuclear bombers in order to make space for an additional 21 Douglas A-4 Skyhawk light attack jets from the US Marines – far more useful in close-air support of an amphibious landing.

On October 22, President Kennedy announced a 'quarantine' on military equipment entering Cuba; effectively a blockade on the island, but the latter term was avoided because it was a de facto act of war under international law.

Enterprise joined Task Force 135, which also included the Forrestal-class supercarrier *Independence* (CVA 62), with the responsibility of round-the-clock early warning patrols over the Windward Passage, the strait between Cuba and Hispaniola. The carriers of TF 135 were also responsible for protecting the US enclave on Cuba if it was attacked. The carriers were themselves at risk from Soviet submarines and from Luna-M rockets and Il-28 *Beagle* bombers based on Cuba.

On October 30, Kennedy agreed to relax the 'quarantine' although the carrier forces continued to

shadow shipping, and the situation remained highly tense. On November 5, two MiG-21 fighters intercepted a flight of VFP-62 Crusaders. The reconnaissance aircraft turned towards the MiGs and lit their afterburners, leading to a five minute stern chase. The MiGs did not fire and the RF-8As escaped.

Enterprise remained on station to police a tentative agreement once it had been struck, and as of the middle of November, naval aircraft had flown 30,000 hours in support of USN operations relating to the Cuban Missile Crisis. *Enterprise* was relieved on December 5 by *Saratoga*, and the confrontation did not truly lift until the middle of the month.

On paper, the conclusion of the Cuban Missile Crisis was equally favourable to both sides, as while the USSR withdrew its plans to install missiles on Cuba, the US agreed to do the same with its missiles in Turkey. The latter agreement, however, was kept secret, so the world largely saw the result as the USSR backing down, and the crisis precipitated the fall of Nikita Khrushchev some years later.

Cowboys and Cossacks

The Cold War stand-off across the world's oceans often developed into a game of 'chicken' that featured plenty of risk to life and limb, even as both sides held back from combat. Both sides systematically monitored each other's activities, while attempting to prevent their opponents from learning too much about their own, and this brought carrier-based aircraft into the front line.

The line as to where legitimate reconnaissance, demonstrations and warnings became excessive aggression was a fuzzy one, which on occasion resulted in loss of life. Naval formations on one side would typically be shadowed by vessels from the other, more or less openly, by submarines, surface warships, specialist reconnaissance vessels posing as civilians, and aircraft.

LEFT: A Sea Vixen FAW2 from *Ark Royal* escorts a Tupolev Tu-95 *Bear* as it attempts to monitor NATO Exercise Straight Laced in the Norwegian Sea on August 25, 1966.
Author's collection

LEFT: A Phantom FGR1 of 892 Squadron prepares to take off from HMS *Ark Royal* during NATO Exercise 'Strong Express' on September 23, 1972, off the coast of Norway, while the Soviet hydrographic survey ship *Nakhodka* maintains a watching brief.
Author's collection

BELOW: The Soviet Kotlin-class destroyer *Nastoychivy* in close company with the carrier HMS *Ark Royal* in October 1970, framed by the tail of 809 Squadron Blackburn Buccaneer S2 XT293. The following month, another ship of this class, the *Bravyy*, collided with *Ark Royal* in the Mediterranean, leading to safer rules on Cold War monitoring activities at sea.
Author's collection

In November 1960, an early face-off involved the Soviet nautical research vessel *Vityaz*, which unlike many USSR 'survey ships' was typically engaged in peaceful scientific studies. Her crew reported being 'buzzed' in the Arabian Sea by a Grumman S-2 Tracker anti-submarine aircraft from USS *Essex*. The USN insisted that the aircraft had simply been trying to establish vessel's identity.

In the early 1960s, the monitoring was not as intensive as it later became. HMS *Ark Royal* noted that in the 1963 NATO Spring Exercises: "the Russians had carried out a very full surveillance of our manoeuvres," leading to high press interest and six journalists sailing with the carrier for the 1964's manoeuvres. But "In the event, the Russian surveillance proved a »

disappointing story, with only our friend the Trawler appearing on the first day and an aircraft sighted briefly on the fourth."

The game of aircraft 'buzzing' carriers turned deadly on May 25, 1968. USS *Essex* was conducting routine anti-submarine flying in the Norwegian Sea when she was approached by a Tupolev Tu-16R, the typical adversary of NATO carriers. The Tu-16 twice passed extremely close to the carrier, on one occasion possibly even overflying the aft flight deck, and on another flying parallel to the carrier at roughly the level of the flight deck.

An S-2 pilot about to launch was told to hold, and recalls seeing the top of the *Badger*'s tail fin sailing past. A helicopter mechanic recalled: "You could feel the heat and smell the jet exhaust."

No doubt to the crew's relief, the Tu-16 moved away, but stayed low to the water. Horrified onlookers saw the port wingtip dip, possibly as the pilot attempted to make a visual check on the carrier and clip the water. The bomber cartwheeled and smashed into the surface. *Essex* immediately dispatched plane-guard helicopters to the scene but found only debris. There were no survivors. The tension increased when a second Tu-16 appeared, to see the carrier and nearby, a column of smoke on the water with helicopters close by.

The pilot of the crashed Tu-16, Lieutenant Colonel Alexander Zakharovich Pliev, was an experienced reconnaissance pilot, reportedly well-versed in 'force demonstration' low-level flights.

The incident came at a time of high wariness between the two sides. Earlier that year, one Soviet and one US submarine had been lost, potentially in the presence of each other's naval forces (although the loss of USS *Scorpion* mere days before the *Essex* incident was not widely known at the time).

The USN was at pains to point out to the USSR that it had not shot down the Tu-16 and submitted

cine film footage of the 'buzzing' as evidence.

The close encounters continued – both sides were concerned about the dangers but neither wished to concede an advantage.

Matters came to a head on November 9, 1970, when the Kotlin-class destroyer *Bravyy* collided with the carrier *Ark Royal* while the latter was transiting to a NATO exercise in the Mediterranean. Soviet shadowers would often attempt to make life difficult for NATO carriers by cutting across the stern while they were recovering aircraft, or across the bow when they were launching. On this occasion, the destroyer cut it too close while *Ark* was flying off 892 Squadron Phantoms, and the carrier struck the warship on the port quarter. Seven Soviet sailors (plus a dog) were thrown overboard, and two sailors were killed.

This was the prompt for both sides to enter into negotiations on an agreement to moderate their conduct during 'surveillance'. Poignantly, among the naval officers involved in the discussions was Captain Edward Day, operations officer on board *Essex* during the episode with the Tu-16, and Soviet Deputy Chief of Staff for Naval Aviation Nikolai I. Vishensky, whose son had been one of the aviators killed that day.

The subsequent agreement remained in place for the remainder of the Cold War. Nevertheless, monitoring continued, often intently, and when the USSR finally obtained its own aircraft carriers in the mid-1970s, with the Kiev-class vertical take-off and landing ships, they were themselves subject to close scrutiny by western forces.

'Whale' Hunting

The development of Electronic Intelligence and Signals Intelligence gathering, usually abbreviated in Western militaries as ELINT and SIGINT, was a key weapon for both sides in the Cold War. This had particular significance for naval aviation, as aircraft were ideal platforms for collecting ELINT and SIGINT, especially on fleets and individual warships far out at sea.

ELINT became a priority for the US Navy during World War Two when radar gained in significance. While radar could detect incoming aircraft, its emissions could in turn be a source of information, for example on enemy air defences and the disposition of ships. When the Cold War began, the increasing sophistication of electronic sensors further increased the value of ELINT.

With the outbreak of war in Korea, the USN formed Fleet Air Reconnaissance squadrons for the Pacific (VQ-1) and Atlantic (VQ-2), which flew daily ELINT missions against the USSR and allied countries. In the 1950s, the USN generally used long-range land-based aircraft for this role, but they could be vulnerable to enemy fighters, as demonstrated when PB4Y2 Privateer 'Turbulent Turtle' was shot down by Soviet aircraft over the Baltic in April 1950, followed by another five aircraft lost over the first half of the decade, mostly to accidents or poor weather but occasionally to hostile aircraft.

One solution was a carrier-based aircraft of higher performance than the lumbering land-based aircraft. By the mid-1950s, the Douglas A-3 Skywarrior bomber was beginning to be outmoded in its primary nuclear strike role. It was capacious enough to fit a variety of sensors, and being carrier-based, could be deployed globally with no need for airbases. The twin jet-powered 'Whale,' as its crews nicknamed it, was faster with a higher ceiling than the US Navy's piston-engined, land-based patrol bombers, and after its initial adaptation to ELINT as the EA-3B, quickly proved its worth.

The two Fleet Reconnaissance Squadrons operated EA-3Bs, both from land bases and detachments aboard carriers. VQ-2 had a permanent land base at Rota in Spain, from where operations around the Mediterranean, Atlantic and across Europe could be staged, and detachments with carrier air groups extended the squadron's reach still further. VQ-2 occasionally provided aircraft and crews to the Pacific, such as during the Cuban Missile Crisis, when ELINT and SIGINT on Soviet forces was in high demand.

The capabilities of the 'Whale' led to it being sought-after from the time of its introduction in 1956 to as late as the first Gulf War in 1991. Unfortunately, the high tempo of operations added to the existing difficulties with the large, unwieldy 'Whale' resulted in a high accident rate, especially when operating from carriers, not least as flights often had to take place at night or in poor weather. The last USN casualties of the Cold War were the seven crewmembers of VQ-2 EA-3B #144850 *Ranger 12*, killed when the aircraft crashed off the flight deck of USS *Nimitz* in the Mediterranean on January 25, 1987.

BELOW: A Douglas EA-3B Skywarrior ELINT aircraft of USN fleet reconnaissance squadron VQ-2 based at Rota, Spain, in August 1976. The ventral 'canoe' containing sensors and electronic equipment was unique to this variant of the 'Whale'.
Ray Thompson

McDONNELL DOUGLAS F-4 PHANTOM II

When it became clear that McDonnell's F3H Demon would be a disappointment, the company turned its attentions to an aircraft that would outstrip the Demon in every area. Despite an initial lack of interest from the US Navy, McDonnell's instincts inspired the iconic carrier jet of the postwar era, a fighter that could do just about anything – the Phantom II.

ABOVE: Phantom FG.1 XT863 of 767 Squadron, the Fleet Air Arm Phantom training unit, RNAS Yeovilton, in 1969. The nose of this aircraft still exists at a scrapyard on the Isle of Wight. Pete West/Key Publishing

BELOW: The first prototype Phantom, the YF4H-1, as it appeared at the time of its first flight. Early production versions would retain its short nose, low cockpit and curved intake lips before the definitive shape was arrived at. Author's collection

In 1953, before the prototype F3H Demon had entered service, it was already clear that the programme was in trouble. The Westinghouse J40 engine that the US Navy (USN) had insisted on was underperforming and late. Meanwhile USN demands to improve armament and range to counter the MiG-15 threat would bring more delays and compromises in other areas.

The McDonnell Aircraft Corporation of St. Louis, Missouri, (later McDonnell Douglas) began to plan more capable developments. There were no immediate prospects for new specifications for naval aircraft, so in August of that year, McDonnell commissioned a study into various potential avenues to evolve the F3H. These ranged from fairly straightforward evolutions with more powerful engines, to more heavily revised twin-engined versions, and still more evolved variants with various new wing planforms, in single- and two-seat options, optimised for a variety of different roles, from interceptor to attack.

On September 19, 1953, McDonnell presented the USN with a proposal for a twin-engined F3H development known internally as Model 98B. The navy rejected the proposal almost straight away. Two supersonic fighters, the Grumman F9F Tiger, and the Vought F8U Crusader, were about to enter service, and the USN's needs were met for the immediate future. Instead, the navy encouraged McDonnell to develop the design for the attack role, as the more urgent need was to replace the service's propeller-driven AD Skyraider and the obsolescent A3D Skywarrior.

McDonnell went back to the drawing board, and also started work on a full-size mockup. The aircraft resembled a more muscular, two-seat F3D, with two engines side-by-side in the mid-fuselage, above a flat delta wing with a 45° sweep at the quarter-chord line.

A year after the initial proposal, the company submitted a revised scheme to the USN. As per the navy's requests, it was heavily skewed towards the air-to-ground mission, with multiple guns and

weapons stations for ordnance. However, just two months later, the USN reconsidered and asked for an emphasis on air-to-air operations. The brief was now for an interceptor, capable of patrolling for two hours in all weathers, with all guns deleted, weapons stations reduced and the main weapon to be the just-introduced AIM-7 Sparrow 2 long-range radar-guided missile. The designation F4H was applied.

Mindful of the difficulties that had beset the F3H thanks to being designed around the problematic J40, McDonnell developed the F4H for both the new General Electric J79 – which offered a considerable advance in power and development potential over existing engines – and the mature Wright J65, already in operation with the US Navy's FJ-3 Fury, and rather smaller and lighter than the J79, but less powerful. The J79 suggested speeds approaching Mach 2 would be possible, compared with around Mach 1.5 for the J65. In April 1955, the USN directed McDonnell to focus their efforts on the J79.

The Phantom Returns

The F4H – it would be redesignated to the familiar F-4 in 1962 when US forces standardised aircraft designations – would include numerous advanced features for the time. This included boundary-layer control on the wing leading edges and flaps (see Rethinking the Carrier), and a search and targeting radar that would operate with the semi-active homing missiles.

Reflecting the extreme stresses both of carrier operations and flight at Mach 2, the airframe was designed with immense strength. Large sections were machined from solid metal instead of built up from smaller parts. Adjustable splitter plates at the intake would govern the radically different air feed at the full range of speeds and altitudes.

The Phantom's aerodynamic controls were unusual, reflecting the careful thinking that went into the design. The Demon experienced wing twist at high speeds so its control system was revised with conventional ailerons working only up to 560kts, above which, spoilers on the inner wing took over. On the Phantom, spoilers were designed in from the start and worked in conjunction with the ailerons. Each aileron only deflected downwards, while the spoiler on the opposite wing provided the equivalent of 'up' aileron, reducing twisting forces on the wing, allowing it to be constructed less heavily, and minimising 'adverse yaw', where an aircraft steers in the opposite direction to a roll. The ailerons also worked as 'flaperons' to reduce landing and take-off speed. All-in-all it was a neat solution for an aircraft that had to handle responsively from Mach 2 right down to stalling speed during carrier landings. An all-moving 'slab' tailplane completed the control surfaces, which were all hydraulically

powered, with artificial feel and automatic stabilisation.

In contrast to the Demon, little needed to be changed during the F4H's design and development phase. The tailplane was given a pronounced anhedral, with the tips angling down, to ensure that it was not blanketed by the wing at any point. Lateral stability needed to be improved, but fortunately here a solution was easy to effect: the outer wing panels could be angled up to provide dihedral at the point where they folded for carrier stowage.

The prototype first flew on May 27, 1958, from Lambert–Saint Louis Airport. Teething issues were addressed for the second flight, when the F4H first went supersonic.

The following year, the name Phantom was chosen, revisiting a previous McDonnell type. The FH-1 Phantom was superseded even by the time of the Korean War, so it may seem surprising that McDonnell would wish to reuse the name so soon, but the 'blink-and-you-miss-it' career of the earlier aircraft meant few eyebrows were raised.

Technically, the new fighter would be the 'Phantom II'.

There was one more hurdle to clear before the Phantom was confirmed for USN service. Vought proposed an evolved version of its successful F8U (later F-8) Crusader, the F8U-3 Crusader III, and the navy insisted on fly-off trials with the Phantom.

The competition was something of a test of concepts as well as the aircraft themselves, the Vought single-seat, single engine aircraft going up against McDonnell's two-seat, twin-engine aircraft. The Crusader III was around three-quarters the all-up weight of the Phantom but had the same fire control radar and missiles.

Although the F8U-3 demonstrated impressive performance and agility, the Phantom prevailed. Flying the F8U-3 while operating the radar led to an unacceptably high work rate for the pilot. With a dedicated Radar Intercept Officer (RIO) and the added reliability of two engines, the Phantom was the best all-round choice, and in December 1958, it was chosen. **»**

ABOVE: An F-4J Phantom of VF-102, USS *Independence*, escorts an Egyptian Air Force Tupolev Tu-16 *Badger* over the eastern Mediterranean on January 12, 1971, during a period of sustained tension in the region. US Navy

BELOW: F-4A Phantom #146817. This was the first aircraft of production block 3, and thus the first to display the classic Phantom shape, with a cockpit raised above the spine of the fuselage for better visibility, and a longer and deeper nose containing the larger AN/APQ-72 radar. Author's collection

PHANTOM DATA

F-4B

Length	19.2m (63ft 0in)
Span	11.7m (38ft 4.5in)
Height	5.0m (16ft 6in)
Empty weight	13,757kg (30,328lb)
Maximum weight	28,030kg (61,795lb)
Range	2,600km (1,615 miles) with external tanks
Service ceiling	60,000ft (18,300m)
Engine	Two × General Electric J79 -GE-8A/-8B/-8C turbojets, 10,900lb dry thrust, 17,000lb with afterburner
Armament	Six × AIM-7 Sparrow and/or 2-4 AIM-9 Sidewinder air-to-air missiles, air-to-surface up to 16,000lb including AGM-45 Shrike, AGM-62 Walleye or AGM-65 Maverick missiles, bombs up to 2,000lb, Reconnaissance and Targeting Pods

PHANTOM TIMELINE

First flight – May 27, 1958
Entry into service – December 1960
First carrier deployment – August 1962
First combat sortie – August 5, 1964
First air combat kill – June 17, 1965
Introduction of F-4J – May 27, 1966
Last USN carrier deployment ends (USN *Midway*) – March 25, 1986
First Royal Navy Phantom Squadron formed – January 1969
Withdrawal from Royal Navy Service – December 15, 1978
Last USN carrier deployment ends (USN *Midway*) – March 25, 1986
Withdrawal from active and reserve USN service – October 1986
Withdrawal of QF-4 target drone from US Navy – September 22, 2004

BELOW: F-4N Phantom #152317 of VF-111 'Sundowners' in USA Bicenntennial markings flies in formation with a US Marine Corps AV-8A Harrier during the six-month evaluation of the VTOL type aboard USS *Roosevelt* in 1976.
Author's collection

Into service

The Phantom went into production quickly but incrementally. After the two prototypes (the first of which was lost in a crash in October 1959), a number of small production blocks followed from 1960, effectively serving as development models to fast-track evaluation.

With the first aircraft of Block 3, #146867, the Phantom finally attained its familiar profile. This machine introduced a new higher cockpit canopy, with greater visibility for the pilot and more headroom for the RIO, with a revised nose containing a larger AN/APQ-72 radar and APA-157 'continuous wave' illuminator. A characteristic 'chin' pod contained an infra-red seeker.

Further, less visible changes were implemented, most notably to the tricky intake splitter plates. Not until the sixth block was the aircraft deemed ready for service. When Tri-Service designations were introduced in 1961, the F4H became the F-4. Retrospectively, development models were designated F-4A, and the service model was dubbed F-4B. This would be one of the major naval variants of the Phantom in addition to the later F-4J which arrived from 1966, and incorporated improvements introduced on US Air Force Phantoms.

Despite being a large and heavy aircraft by the standards of existing carrier fighters, the Phantom handled well and was predictable in deck landing, while the thrust from its two J79s engendered confidence. Squadrons operating types such as the F3H Demon and the Douglas F4D Skyray began switching to the Phantom as soon as there were enough aircraft available. The first Phantom squadron, VF-121, started working up with F-4As as early as December 1960, while the first front line unit, VF-74 qualified for carrier flying less than a year later.

The first carrier deployment took place with VF-74 from August 1962 aboard USS *Forrestal* in the Atlantic Fleet, while the Pacific Fleet gained its first Phantom squadron just a month later with VF-114 aboard USS *Kitty Hawk*.

When the US began its own air strikes in the long-running war between South Vietnam and North Vietnam in 1964, 13 fully carrier-qualified squadrons were equipped with the Phantom. F-4Bs flying from USS *Constellation* were among the aircraft to conduct air strikes in response to the Gulf of Tonkin incident between North Vietnamese and US naval forces.

Phantoms had a slightly rocky start to their combat career in Vietnam, and in the first engagement with MiGs the score was one-all, though it remains uncertain if the Phantom was shot down by a MiG or by 'friendly fire'.

The majority of air-to-air engagements for USN Phantoms came early in the war – there was only one US Navy kill between 1970 and 1972. Phantom crews claimed 40 aircraft shot down for the loss of seven in return over the course of the conflict. As the war dragged on, the USN's F-4s saw more combat in the air–ground role, using the type's high lifting capacity and performance, though their accuracy with basic 'iron' bombs was low. In May 1972, though, the USN saw its heaviest fighting in the air, with 16 MiGs shot down by navy jets, four of them by a single Phantom crew over two days.

Although the F-8 Crusader outperformed the Phantom in the air-to-air role in Vietnam, the advantages of the two-seat type were ever more apparent, and within two years of the US withdrawal from Vietnam, the single-seater had been replaced by Phantoms and the new Grumman F-14.

The Phantom served with the US Navy and Marines into the 1980s, but as it finally began to be superseded by newer types, it continued to be valuable, with many converted to pilotless target drones until withdrawal from USN use in 2004.

CARRIER AIRCRAFT OVER VIETNAM

In 1965, the USA slid into war in Vietnam. The US Navy's carrier aircraft would play a major role in the US prosecution of the conflict to the bitter end.

BELOW: An F-8E of VF-53, USS *Ticonderoga*, flying a mission from Dixie Station over South Vietnam on November 30, 1965, carrying 'Zuni' rockets for ground attack on the fuselage sides.
Author's collection

In August 1964, the so-called Gulf of Tonkin Incident led to direct US military action in the long-running war between the communist People's Republic (North Vietnam) and the Republic (South Vietnam).

At the beginning of sustained air operations by the US Navy (USN), its complement of aircraft was, as it had been in Korea 12 years earlier, a mix of propeller and jet types, many of which were relatively simple. At the end of the conflict eight years later, jets of increasing sophistication were dominant.

On August 2, North Vietnamese torpedo boats responded to US covert operations by attacking the destroyer, USS *Maddox*. President Johnson authorised immediate air strikes against North Vietnamese targets in retaliation, and a few days later, Congress passed a resolution authorising the president to take military action in southeast Asia in support of any friendly country "requesting assistance in defence of its freedom."

In February 1965, an attack on a US military compound led to further air strikes from US Navy (USN) carriers stationed off the east coast. Operation Flaming Dart I targeted

a North Vietnamese (NV) military barracks close to the demilitarised border area (DMZ).

USS *Coral Sea* and *Hancock* launched 49 aircraft against Đồng Hới, with A-4 Skyhawks carrying out the attack with bombs and rockets, and F-8 Crusaders detailed to strafe anti-aircraft gun (AA) emplacements, with RF-8 reconnaissance Crusaders recording the results. The raid was met with heavy anti-aircraft fire (AA) and one A-4 was shot down; the pilot killed.

The attack had been dramatic, but the damage was relatively slight. Nevertheless, insurgents from the National Liberation Front of South Vietnam, known as the Viet Cong (VC) carried out a retaliatory attack on a hotel where US personnel were billeted, leading to Flaming Dart II on February 11, in which 99 aircraft from the three carriers attacked Chánh Hòa barracks, 35 miles north of the DMZ.

This time, the attacking aircraft included A-1 Skyraider propeller

aircraft as well as A-4s, and F-4 Phantoms joined the Crusaders on flak suppression duties. Once again, the AA was intense and this time three aircraft were lost, while others took damage. The pilots survived, though one was captured by NV forces.

The second raid's results were as unimpressive as the first, and they had no deterrent effect on NV actions. President Johnson was persuaded to approve a much larger scale programme of air interdiction against NV communication routes, aiming to strangle reinforcement and resupply, in the hope of forcing North Vietnam into an accommodation.

Yankee and Dixie

The series of strikes known as Operation Rolling Thunder began in March 1965, and marked the start of the US's long term, overt military involvement in the Vietnam conflict.

US carriers were now on station permanently off the east coast at location Point Y, or Yankee in the NATO phonetic alphabet, which became known as Yankee Station.

In May US Army General Westmoreland requested an additional carrier station further south. This became known as 'Dixie Station' in a joking reference to the Southern US as a counterpart to the 'Yankees' in the north. Westmoreland's request indicated how far the USN had come in providing close support since Korea (see Carrier Jets over Korea) when differences in doctrine and poor communication led to army-navy relations breaking down. In the early

months of operations in Vietnam, the USN's air support of infantry operations were so impressive that the army effectively asked for it to be expanded.

Rolling Thunder sorties from Yankee Station began on March 18, with a strike from *Coral Sea* and *Hancock* against a supply depot. The intention was for strikes behind NV lines, starting in the vicinity of the DMZ, advancing over time to the environs of Hanoi, in the hope that the threat to the capital would persuade North Vietnam to negotiate for peace.

However, US operations were hampered from the start by rigid rules of engagement imposed by Washington. All strikes had to have prior approval, and preceding photographic reconnaissance was forbidden, as were follow-up strikes and use of unexpended ordnance on targets of opportunity. Attacks on settlements were restricted. These rules limited the damage by each attack and made it easier for NV forces to mitigate them.

By contrast, Dixie Station was not subject to the same restrictions. As its purpose was to provide close air support to ground forces, USN squadrons did not require prior approval for each operation and could act with far greater flexibility. At the same time, operations in the south tended to face less opposition, particularly in the form of the intense AA that was typically experienced over the north. As a result, air wings arriving in theatre tended to be assigned to Dixie Station first, to get used to the nature of operations »

ABOVE:
The catapult officer signals for an A-4 Skyhawk to launch from the starboard catapult of USS *Coral Sea*, during operations in the South China Sea, March 24, 1965. US Navy, USN 1111691-A

while facing only relatively light opposition.

Rolling Thunder appeared to be eroding NV ability to move supplies and troops to the front, but in reality, they only made NV forces alter their routes and procedures to avoid the raids, transporting men and materiel at night and parking vehicles in villages during the day where they could not be attacked under the US rules of engagement.

US attack aircraft ranged from the small, 16,000lb Douglas A-4 Skyhawk single seat, single engine attack jet, to the large Douglas A-3 Skywarrior, a multi-place strategic nuclear bomber with a 70,000lb gross weight. The Skyhawk was developed specifically for close support, based on experiences in Korea, and lacked features such as radar and sophisticated navigation equipment. This meant the pilot had to visually identify targets and relied on guidance to and from the target. Fighters were the single-engined, single-seat F-8 Crusader, and the twin-engined, two-seat F-4 Phantom, while reconnaissance was typically carried out by RF-8 Crusaders or the larger and more sophisticated North American RA-5 Vigilante.

Resistance intensifies

The early air strikes had been opposed by AA weapons such as 37mm cannon, and small arms. Soon after operations began, evidence of dramatic strengthening of air defences became apparent. Photographs from a reconnaissance Crusader from USS *Coral Sea* taken on April 5, provided the first proof that Soviet-built S-75 Desna (NATO name *Guideline*) surface-to-air missiles (SAM) were arriving in theatre.

Initially, permission to attack S-75 sites was refused. However, this changed when several US aircraft were shot down, a USAF Phantom in July 1965, while the first navy aircraft lost to the missiles were several A-4s from USS *Midway* the following month. The response was Operation Iron Hand, which began on August 12. The result was a frustrating and largely fruitless hunt for missile launch sites which did not produce results for another two months, when navy Skyhawks finally located and bombed launchers north of the capital.

Visual searches for the sites were clearly ineffective, not least because any aircraft stumbling across a site

was at serious risk of being shot down. The USN moved to electronic surveillance in an attempt to detect the missiles' targeting radar, with the USN adapting obsolescent A-3 Skywarriors into EA-3 aircraft for the role (see Cold War Confrontation), and the USMC adopted the antiquated Douglas Skynight night fighter (See Carrier Jets Over Korea) as the EF-10. When the EA-3s and EF-10s pinpointed a targeting radar, the location would be marked for a strike, which had to be carried out with precise navigation in a tricky approach at low level.

North Vietnamese resistance to US air operations was not restricted to SAMs. The Vietnam People's Air Force (VPAF) was chiefly active in the air transport role prior to large-scale US involvement. However, pilots had been training in China and in 1962, the first North Vietnamese pilots qualified on the MiG-17. The VPAF still had no fighters of its own but in February 1964, the USSR gifted North Vietnam MiG-17s, with which it formed the 921st Fighter Regiment.

Although the MiG-17 was somewhat dated by the standards of 1965, as a subsonic fighter with no radar and the primary weapon of guns, its

BELOW: An F-8E Crusader launches from USS *Bon Homme Richard* in a vortex of catapult steam, on Yankee Station in the Gulf of Tonkin, 24 May 1967.
Author's collection

RIGHT: Grumman A-6A Intruder #154126 at the Greenham Common Air Tattoo in 1976, when it was the personal aircraft of VA-176's executive officer, USS *America*. This aircraft was assigned to VA-85 'Black Falcons' in 1968 when it deployed on *America* to Yankee Station.
Ray Thompson

BELOW: F-4J Phantom #158372 of VF-21 'Freelancers' USS *Ranger* during a training flight with 25lb practice bombs under the Sidewinder rails. VF-21 switched to the F-4J model Phantom in 1968 and made numerous deployments to Vietnam aboard *Ranger* from 1968 to 1971.
Author's collection

arrival in theatre threw US forces off balance. Crusaders from VF-211 (USS *Hancock*) were the first US aircraft to encounter VPAF MiG-17s, on April 3, during a large raid on Thanh Hóa Bridge, and one of the F-8s was damaged. The following day a VPAF MiG claimed its first US aerial victory, over a US Air Force F-105. Five days after that, a USN Phantom was downed in an engagement with MiG-17s over the Gulf of Tonkin, though it may have been the victim of friendly fire.

Though the MiG was slower and less well armed than US fighters, it was more manoeuvrable, and its guns were more effective in a close-in dogfight than missiles, which were the only weapon available to types such as the USN's F-4B. Poor performance of US missiles exacerbated this problem.

The situation only got worse for US aircrews when short-ranged but fast MiG-21s began to arrive in 1966. With intelligent direction from ground controllers, the supersonic Mig-21s were able to work with MiG-17s in co-ordinated attacks on US strikes. The first USN kill of a MiG-21 was made on October 9, 1966, when Commander Richard Bellingham, commanding officer of VF 162, in an F-8 from USS *Oriskany*, scored a Sidewinder hit as the MiG attempted to attack a strike force from another carrier.

Proficiency in air combat had fallen to a low priority in the USN and USAF, due to the belief that the dogfight was a thing of the past. The sobering experience against a handful of North Vietnamese jets flown by pilots with little experience led to a rapid reappraisal. New tactics were developed to allow US pilots to play to the strengths of their aircraft while mitigating the strengths of aircraft like the MiG-17. Guns were reintroduced to types that lacked them.

In fact, USN aircraft only scored four 'gun kills' against MiGs »

during the war and two of these were by A-1 Skyraiders, taking opportunistic shots when attacking MiGs that had overshot. The other two were scored by F-8 Crusaders. One A-4 pilot even managed to score a victory over a MiG-17 with Zuni ground attack rockets on May 1, 1967.

Overall, though, the performance of USN fighters against nominally inferior opposition in Vietnam led to the establishment of the US Navy Fighter Weapons School, popularly known as TOPGUN, in 1968. By the end of hostilities in 1973, the USN had a success rate of 3.68:1 against MiGs, compared with 2.04 for the USAF.

Rethinking and Renewal

In 1965, the first full year of USN air operations in Vietnam, 82 aircrew were killed, missing or in captivity, and over 100 aircraft had been lost, and as operations paused from Christmas until the end of January 1966, the USN had little to show for its efforts.

Rolling Thunder failed to push North Vietnam to the negotiating table and did not even have an appreciable effect on the movement of supplies. The rapid strengthening of AA defences increased losses and reduced successes still further. Pilots typically flew 16–22 sorties a month over North Vietnam, with the most

active pilots flying closer to 30. At this level of activity, the chances of individual pilots being shot down was dangerously high.

It was particularly so for the reconnaissance crews. Low-level photo reconnaissance was typically carried out by RF-8 Crusaders, while medium-altitude photography was handled by the larger and more complex RA-5 Vigilante. Their chief responsibility was photographing targets after they had been hit to assess damage, and this predictable

pattern made them highly vulnerable. The RA-5's sophisticated suite of cameras provided excellent intelligence, though was difficult to maintain on a carrier on station, and the medium altitude flights were easier to target.

At least USN crews could look forward to newer and more capable aircraft beginning to arrive – the end was finally in sight for the piston-engined propeller types.

In November 1965, the turboprop Grumman E-2A Hawkeye began

ABOVE: LTV A-7E Corsair II of VA-192 being prepared for aboard USS *Kitty Hawk* for a strike somewhere in Vietnam in 1971. The aircraft is armed with Mk 82 general purpose bombs and an AGM-95A Shrike anti-radar missile. Author's collection

LEFT: A-7A Corsair IIs on a training mission from Point Mugu, California with reserve squadron VA-305 in 1972, as the Vietnam conflict was winding down. US Navy, via Ray Thompson

to supersede the E-1B Tracer in the airborne warning and control role, with far greater capability in detecting threats and directing aircraft in response to them.

Throughout 1965, the propeller driven A-1 Skyraider was still the main medium attack aircraft in the air wings of most carriers on Yankee Station. From June, the new Grumman A-6 Intruder began to arrive in theatre.

The A-6 was roughly equivalent to the British Blackburn Buccaneer (see pages 44-45), a twin-engined low-level all-weather strike aircraft with a formidable payload and sophisticated systems, designed to operate at high subsonic speeds. VA-75 arrived with the new type aboard USS *Independence* and within weeks was flying sorties south of Hanoi.

Within three years, the venerable 'Spad,' as the A-1 was nicknamed, would be entirely replaced in the strike role. »

ABOVE: Vought RF-8G #144623 of VFP-63 Detachment 43, USS *Coral Sea*, over Vietnam on July 27, 1967, the day after the deployment began. Reconnaissance missions in Vietnam were risky – on September 21, this aircraft was lost to AA fire, the pilot Lieutenant Commander Milton Vescelius was killed. Author's collection

LEFT: RF-8G of VFP-62 Detachment 38, "Sooper Snoopers," USS *Shangri La*, being readied for a mission over Vietnam in 1964–65. Author's collection

RIGHT: North American RA-5C Vigilante reconnaissance aircraft on approach to land on USS *Constellation* off the coast of North Vietnam in May 1972. On deck are an EA-3 electronic surveillance Skywarrior and an F-4J Phantom.
Author's collection

BELOW: An RA-5C Vigilante undergoing maintenance on the flight deck of USS *Independence* in the South China Sea during operations off Vietnam in December 1965. The multi-mode radar in the nose is in view, as is the clear blister beneath the nose which houses the television camera for the inertial navigation system. The retractable in-flight refuelling probe is extended.
Author's Collection

The A-6's long range and enormous payload of 18,000lb together with advanced radar and computers for navigation and weapon delivery made it a powerful asset in the USN's armoury. It was the first type to carry out strikes with the target entirely located by the aircraft's own radar. As it operated at very low level, however, the A-6 could be vulnerable to small-arms fire – of the 84 Intruders shot down during combat over Vietnam, 56 fell to ground fire.

The Ling-Temco-Vought A-7 Corsair II light attack aircraft reached Vietnam towards the end of 1967 when VA-147 arrived on the returning USS *Ranger*. This aircraft was developed to replace the A-4 Skyhawk, which was beginning to seem too basic and limited in its development potential for the USN, though the USMC continued with the type until the mid-1980s.

The A-7's development was astonishingly rapid for a combat aircraft in the 1960s, with the contract issued in March 1964, first flight in September 1965, delivery of production aircraft in October 1966, clearance for operations in February 1967, and first combat sorties on December 4 that year. It was derived from the Vought F-8, and the intention was for considerable commonality, but in reality, the A-7 was a completely new type, with the

main undercarriage the only major element carried over. This makes its rapid entry into service all the more remarkable, though it would take a few more years for the really effective variants to appear. The 'Short Little Ugly Fella' (the last word often replaced by a cruder alternative) offered a major improvement in accuracy, thanks to its Doppler navigation system and integrated weapons computer, while it was quick to turn around between missions, required low maintenance, and had excellent fuel economy.

It was relatively slow when fully laden, however, and early versions were considered underpowered. It was, though, particularly safe. VA-147 lost their first A-7 just 18 days after their introduction to combat but did not lose another in the next 1,400 sorties.

Escalation

In 1966 with the conflict bogged down, President Johnson relented to demands to reduce target restrictions. Johnson had been resistant to allowing air strikes in or near areas of high population. This included oil and petrochemical infrastructure in the northeast of Vietnam. On June 29, A-4s flying from USS *Ranger* bombed the Haiphong oil storage facility, reportedly doing heavy damage.

That year, Yankee Station was moved further north, reflecting the increasingly aggressive approach to attacks throughout the country. In an echo of the Korean War, a new focus on transport communications with a focus on bridge-busting took place, once again trying to cut off NV forces' ability to supply the front line.

This programme was just as frustrating as Rolling Thunder, as it quickly became apparent that North Vietnamese engineers were capable of quickly rebuilding damaged bridges. The volume with which supplies and weapons were now pouring into North Vietnam from the USSR and China made the results of attacks seem like a drop in the ocean.

The fact was that attacks with 'dumb bombs' were rarely accurate enough to do much damage, and while aircraft with more sophisticated targeting systems such as the A-6 and A-7 were able to do better, too many missions were being flown by aircraft such as the Phantom and Skyhawk.

Meanwhile, the VPAF was having some success in directing its MiGs against USAF bombers while avoiding US fighters. Operation Bolo at the beginning of 1967 was a fighter sweep reminiscent of the ones carried out over Germany in 1944. A formation of F-4s effectively posed as a flight of F-105s on a bombing mission. When attacked by MiGs, they turned the tables and shot down seven MiG-21s. The VPAF was believed to only have 12 of the modern jets left and appeared to withdraw them to consider tactics and training, but the USSR supplied more before long.

Another new tactic in early 1967 was the use of A-6s to lay mines in rivers. For the most part though, the overall prosecution of the war differed little from 1965, with no real sense of how it might bring victory closer. A partial halt on bombing began in early 1968, which became a full halt in November, though air strikes continued against communist forces in South Vietnam.

A phased withdrawal of US forces took place throughout 1969–70 and USN aircraft dropped no bombs on North Vietnam until 1972, while there were only sporadic encounters with VPAF fighters.

A flurry of engagements in early 1972 led to some USN pilots, early graduates of the TOPGUN programme, racking up impressive aerial combat scores and vindicating the new training approach.

In March 1972, North Vietnamese forces drove through the DMZ in a full invasion of the South. The phased withdrawal meant the USN only had two carriers on station, and four others were rushed to the theatre.

The final aerial offensive of the war, Operation Linebacker, finally seemed to be having an effect, and the river mining operations gravely hampered supply lines. However, this was suspended when peace talks began, and the pause was used by North Vietnam to rebuild its defences and supplies. The failure of talks led to a second massive bombing assault in December, with commensurately heavy losses in aircrews, including A-6s attacking SAM sites to help protect the USAF's B-52s.

North Vietnam re-entered peace talks at the end of the year, and on January 23, 1973, a ceasefire was announced, the same day as an F-4 was shot down by AA fire at Quảng Trị – the last USN aircraft loss of the war. Operations continued over Cambodia and Laos, but these, too, ended in June 1973, while the majority of US forces withdrew. South Vietnam fell to a renewed assault in 1975, and USN aircraft covered the evacuation of US citizens in April.

BELOW: F-4B Phantom #153006 of VF-154, USS *Ranger*, drops its bombs on an artillery site north of the demilitarised zone, in support of the 3rd Marine division, February 1968. Naval History and Heritage Command, USN 1117963

TODAY

EXCLUSIVE REPORT | THE UNSUNG CONCORDE
Test pilot's memories of 'Delta Golf'

March 2024
Issue No 011,
Vol 52, No 3

AEROPLANE
HISTORY IN THE AIR SINCE 1911

SPITFIRE
from the subcontinent

Stunning new look for ex-Indian warbird

FREE GIFT
WORTH £25.00!

BATTLE OF BERLIN
The RAF's offensive: success or failure?

BEDSHEET BOMBER
Restoring a movie star Mitchell

THE MUSTANG FAMILY
Three generations of P-51 pilots

Aeroplane is still providing the best aviation coverage around. With focus on iconic military aircraft from the 1930s to the 1960s.

shop.keypublishing.com/amsubs

BUMPER 100-PAGE ISSUE! | FREE 2024 AVIATION EVENTS GUIDE

AVIATION NEWS
The past, present and future of flight   www.Key.Aero

BACK TO SQUARE ONE
Can Boeing regain airline and passenger trust after another MAX incident?

WIDEBODY AMBITION
Flydubai's Dreamliner deal in detail

TOWARDS A NEW MILLENNIUM
RNLAF transitions from C-130 to MC-390

FREE GIFT
WORTH £8.99!

RN FLANK
...ies and F-16s

...EUM / HAVANA 1995 / DUTCH STARFIGHTER
... OPS INTERVIEW / REGISTER REVIEW

March 2024   £5.60

Aviation News is renowned for providing the best coverage of every branch of aviation.

shop.keypublishing.com/ansubs

hing.com

CRISIS POINT

Originally a purely military asset, the jet age saw the carrier become a political one too. When tensions rose anywhere in the world, aircraft carriers would not be far away.

ABOVE: SNCASE Aquilon SE.202 of the Aéronavale over the Alps. Author's collection

The aircraft carrier started out as a tool of war but in the jet age found a new occupation helping to maintain peace – or at least, that was the theory. As a means of transporting military capability anywhere in the world, the carrier had remarkable capacity to influence world events at great distances.

Carrier responses took place in most major regions of the world, but the hottest spots were the Caribbean, the Mediterranean and the Far East.

From the end of World War Two in 1945 to the dissolution of the Soviet Union in 1991, US carrier forces were involved in at least 140 responses to international incidents and crises, not counting deployments in Vietnam and Korea. To this can be added the similar responses and the collaborative operations with the other carrier navies. Most crisis responses ended after a matter of days, but in some cases, carrier forces were involved for years.

The catalysts for carrier deployments included revolutions, coups, and other disturbances, in case unrest spilled into wider violence; threats of waters being closed to shipping, to enforce the right of free navigation; buildups of military forces that presaged invasion; and reacting to terrorist activities.

Out of Africa

The first jets of the French Navy's air arm, the Aéronavale, were involved in an international incident almost as soon as they entered service.

French efforts to create a domestic naval jet fighter failed in the early 1950s (see 'Early Steps') resulting in a search for a ready-made, radar-equipped, all-weather fighter, with attack capability, from overseas. The jet chosen was the de Havilland Sea Venom, licence-built by SNCASE as the Aquilon – a twin-boom two-seater,

fully navalised with arresting and catapult gear, and folding wings.

French variants included the two-seat SE.202, with an American Westinghouse AN/APQ-65 radar in the nose, and the single-seat SE.203, with the AN/APQ-94 radar. They were armed with Matra 511 air-to-air missiles and Nord AA.20 air-to-surface missiles.

Deliveries of the carrier-capable versions began in April 1956, too late to take part in the Suez operations (see 'End of Empire'). Flottille 16F was formed in January 1955, under the command of Lieutenant Vaisseau Georges Picchi, the first French pilot to deck-land a Sea Venom. The second unit, 11F, followed in April. They worked up with land-based Venoms before the carrier types were delivered.

France's existing carriers were not adapted to operate jets, so the Aquilons had to wait until the new ships, *Clemenceau*, and *Foch*, were ready before they could go to sea.

In the meantime, 16F and 11F were dispatched to Algeria.

For some years, the country had been divided between those who craved independence and French-born Algerians determined to remain under French control. By 1958, militant separatist groups were active, and 11F was transferred to Maison Blanche near Algiers as part of an increase in air power. The squadron flew ground attack operations with 20mm cannon and rockets for three months, before being relieved by 16F, which did the same.

The French military won the war but lost the peace. International pressure, falling support at home and recognition that the situation was untenable persuaded France to submit to independence in July 1962.

France maintained other colonial possessions in Africa, including a military base at Bizerte, Tunisia, which the Tunisian government wanted rid of, and in July 1961 a blockade of the port began. The two Aquilon squadrons were transferred there in September, attacking Tunisian positions with guns and rockets. Again, the French military succeeded in their actions but the

international opposition to France's actions led to a ceasefire and France's withdrawal from the base.

The new carrier *Clemenceau* had arrived by now, and in December, 11F and 16F carried out deck-landing training.

Within a few years, the Aquilon was replaced by the Étendard IV M and Vought F-8E Crusader. French pilots experienced the Vought during a cross-decking exercise in 1962, and the Aéronavale ordered a version tailored to French needs. The Crusader had an unusual high-lift device – the entire wing changed its angle of attack for take-off and landing, creating lift without the nose rising and blocking the pilot's view. This worked well on USN carriers, but the smaller French hulls required the addition of boundary-layer control (see 'Rethinking the Carrier') on the flaps.

French F-8Es were wired to carry the Matra M530 air-to-air missile as well as Sidewinders and four 20mm cannon, they were also equipped with AN/APQ-104 radar.

Crusaders flying from *Clemenceau* took part in Operation Saphir I in 1974–75 and Saphir II in Djibouti in

1977. These were huge 'show of force' exercises by the combined French military to ensure that a pro-French government was not dislodged by anti-French liberation movements in the transition to independence.

The only confirmed interception by a French Crusader took place during Saphir II in 1977 when a two-ship training dogfight against two Armée de l'Air F-100 Super Sabres almost went horribly wrong. The Crusaders intercepted what they took to be the F-100s, only to realise they were actually Yemeni MiG-21s, carrying air-to-air missiles. The Crusaders went 'weapons hot,' but the MiGs did not engage, and the fighters returned home, relieved.

Blue Bat

The Suez Crisis seemed to confirm US fears that the Soviet Union was building a new 'sphere of influence' in the eastern Mediterranean, and that Arab nations were steadily becoming more anti-West.

On July 14, 1958, Arab nationalists overthrew the British puppet government of Iraq. Fearing a spread of such revolutions across the Arab world, the pro-Western President ➤➤

BELOW: Vought F-8E Crusader of the Aéronavale, known to the crews as the 'Crouze', launching from USS *Shangri-La* during carrier qualification trials for French squadrons. The first French Crusader squadron to activate was Flottille 12F in October 1964.
Author's collection

Chamoun of Lebanon requested US, British, and French military support, informing them of rioting, rebel groups in Beirut, and Syrian partisans entering the country. King Hussein of Jordan also asked the UK for military aid, so it was suggested that the British cover Jordan, while the US handled Lebanon.

The US Operation 'Blue Bat' handily demonstrated the usefulness of carrier groups. Two US Army battle groups were available, but air transport to bring them to Lebanon was not. US Air Force combat jets to support them had to transit from the US, requiring a massive logistical operation taking days or even weeks. The three aircraft carriers in the Mediterranean, USS *Essex*, *Wasp,* and *Saratoga*, meanwhile, prepared to sail within hours.

US Marines were on the beach within 20 hours of the President's request, as FJ-4 Furies and AD Skyraiders from *Essex* roared overhead – the jets had flown ahead of the carrier and refuelled at Cyprus.

It was an impressive display which caused any inclination to revolt to melt away. *Essex* maintained a constant air-umbrella with her aircraft for the next nine days, with the self-contained maintenance, armaments, fuel, and operations facilities that represented the aircraft carrier's great advantage. It took the USAF and army five days before the first elements arrived.

The Royal Navy carrier in the region was HMS *Eagle* which, unluckily, had put into Malta at the start of the month for maintenance. The ship put to sea, despite some damaged boilers, and made for Cyprus for a conference between the local military commanders. *Eagle*'s diarist recorded: "We were to be responsible for the provision of air cover for our troops going to Jordan over the southern part of the route from Cyprus to Amman. We went to full war stations, lifebelts and anti-flash gear were issued, and all wore protective clothing." *Eagle* carried Hawker Sea Hawks, de Havilland Sea Venoms, and Fairey Gannets, and she took up station off Haifa, joined by the Sea Hawks of 802 Squadron,

recently disembarked from *Ark Royal* and recalled from leave. Over five days, her aircraft flew exactly 500 sorties, 250 of them cover for the air transport and the rest for other purposes such as anti-submarine searches. One of *Eagle*'s fighters' responsibilities was protecting the stream of civilian airliners evacuating US nationals out of Beirut.

Eagle withdrew to Cyprus for replenishment when the evacuation ended on July 22, and was briefly relieved by HMS *Albion*.

Taiwan Strait

When the nationalist government of China was overthrown by the Chinese Communist Party in 1949, Chiang Kai-shek and millions of supporters fled to the island of Taiwan. They formed the Republic of China (ROC), which the US recognised as the legitimate government, while the communists founded the rival People's Republic of China (PRC). The USN sent the 7th Fleet to ensure the waters between Taiwan and mainland China, the Taiwan Strait, remained neutral territory.

The republic continued to control a number of small islands along the mainland coast, including the Quemoy, Matsu, and Tachen groups, and in August 1954 deployed troops to start building fortifications there.

LEFT: F-14B Tomcat of VF-84 'Jolly Rogers' preparing to launch from USS *Nimitz*. Aircraft from this squadron intercepted a pair formidable MiG-25 fighters off the Libyan coast in 1981. Ray Thompson

The PRC responded with a heavy artillery bombardment.

By January 1955, the ROC considered the Tachen Islands untenable, and asked the USN for help. Six carriers of Task Force 77 covered the evacuation of 15,000 civilians and 11,000 military personnel.

Diplomatic channels opened between the US and PRC, and for a time the situation eased. In the summer of 1958, however, PRC artillery around Amoy Bay resumed firing on the Quemoy Islands.

On July 14, USS *Lexington*, then conducting deck-landing training

off San Francisco, was ordered to embark her aircraft and join the USS *Hancock* and USS *Shangri-La* in the Taiwan Strait. Across the three carriers, 200 aircraft could be called upon. *Lexington* arrived on August 7.

The US warships patrolled the strait and escorted ROC shipping, triggering a dramatic reduction in the intensity of the bombardment. Before long, US Air Force aircraft arrived at Taiwan, with the support organisation they needed, and the carriers could stand down. It was however, yet another demonstration of how quickly carriers could »

BELOW: 'Cross decking' between US Navy and Fleet Air Arm aircraft in 1957, showing the types used by both services in the Jordan and Lebanon crises the following year – the supersonic F-8 Crusader fighter (centre), and the strictly subsonic straight-wing UK equivalents, Hawker Sea Hawk (left) and DH Sea Venom (centre-low). Author's collection

RIGHT: A Grumman
F-14B Tomcat,
armed with the
type's main
weapon, the long-
range AIM-54
Phoenix missile.
In reality this was
hardly ever used,
and the USN's
only kills with the
Tomcat were made
with the faithful
Sidewinder, seen
above the Phoenix.

Ray Thompson

BELOW: Vought
F-8E Crusaders
of the Aéronavale
in the clouds.
The type was
operated by the
French Navy from
1964 to 1999,
seeing service
during numerous
crisis responses
in Djibouti,
Lebanon, and
the Persian Gulf.

Author's collection

be on scene, fully operational and influencing events.

Mediterranean Heat

Twenty to 30 years after the Suez, Jordan, and Libyan incidents, a second wave of instability rocked the central and eastern Mediterranean. States and terrorist groups, in some cases state-sponsored, began threatening air and sea transport. The Libyan regime of Muammar Qaddafi declared sovereignty over a wide swathe of international waters in the Gulf of Sidra, which the US considered to be a violation of international law, though initially took no action. When Ronald Reagan entered the White House in 1981, he quickly approved a demonstration of US willingness to enforce freedom of navigation, centred around USS *Forrestal* and USS *Nimitz*.

The carriers stayed north of the zone claimed by Libya, while destroyers moved into the gulf, covered by USN aircraft, including the Grumman F-14 Tomcats of VF-14 and VF-84 from *Nimitz*. The F-14 was an air-superiority fighter introduced in the mid-1970s, which had replaced the last F-8 Crusaders and some of the USN's Phantoms. It featured a variable-geometry 'swing wing' and a plethora of modern systems including long-range radar, with the capability to launch the sophisticated AIM-54 Phoenix missile. Reagan authorised USN crews to pursue any Libyan aircraft behaving in a threatening way "All the way to the hangar."

On August 18, a number of Libyan aircraft took off to probe the air patrol. F-14s and F-4s performed 35 interceptions – most of the Libyan aircraft turned back but six entered the patrol zone and were escorted away by the US Navy jets.

The following day, six F-14s and four F-4s took up their patrol stations at first light, guided by an E-2C Hawkeye airborne early warning aircraft. At 0725, the first two-aircraft patrol was due to return when a Tomcat pilot, Commander 'Hank' Kleeman, detected a contact heading towards his station and increasing speed. The pair of Tomcats adopted a combat formation and accelerated. The Libyan contact – actually two Soviet-built Sukhoi Su-22 *Fitter* fighters – continued to close and one launched a K-13 heat-seeking missile.

The K-13 missed, and the Tomcats immediately manoeuvred to engage the Su-22s. The Sukhois tried to flee, but the F-14s each shot one down with a Sidewinder. This was the first

USN air combat since Vietnam and helped weaken Qaddafi's claims of sovereignty over the Gulf of Sidra. Nevertheless, Libya continued to be considered a threat to peace in the region, particularly with Qaddafi's sponsorship of terrorism and rebel movements elsewhere, including Chad. In 1984, France and Libya signed an agreement to de-escalate the situation there. The French carrier *Foch* carried out a demonstration of force off Libya, Operation Mirmillon, to remind Qaddafi of the consequences of breaking the agreement.

To the east, meanwhile, Lebanon erupted into civil war. The UN authorised a peacekeeping force in 1983, which itself became the target of attacks. The USN carriers *Independence* and *Kennedy* were present, as well as the Marine Nationale carriers *Clemenceau* and *Foch* with their Breguet Alizés, F-8E Crusaders and Dassault Super Étendards. Dassaults carried out a reprisal raid against Hezbollah positions at Baalbeck with 250kg and 400kg bombs, with Crusaders escorting, following the bombing of a French barracks.

When Syrian surface-to-air missiles were fired at F-14s flying over Lebanon, strikes on Syrian air defences were approved. These were successful but at the cost of a US Navy A-6 and A-7 being shot down, with the loss of some of their crews. The deployment ended in February 1984.

Persian Gulf

The waters bordered by Iran and the Arabian Peninsula became the scene of increasing tension and confrontation through the 1980s. The Gulf had already been the scene of the British show of force in support of Kuwait in the 1960s (see 'End of Empire') matters reached a head when the long-running Iran-Iraq War spilled over.

Oil tankers and the facilities to load them became strategic targets, leading to ships and sailors of neutral countries being targeted. Sporadic attacks on ships took place from 1984, but in 1987 the situation escalated to such a degree that the USN and Marine Nationale sent carriers and other naval forces to protect tankers, under Operation Earnest Will and Operation Prométhée, respectively.

This led to the longest cruise of the veteran French carrier *Clemenceau*'s career – 14 months away from her home port. Five patrols were made between July 1987 and September 1988, with intensive air activity to dissuade attacks on French-flagged vessels. President Mitterrand gave a lengthy interview from the deck of *Clemenceau*, indicating the importance of 'carrier diplomacy'.

The Iran-Iraq War ended in 1988, but the fallout continued to disrupt the region. Iraq's relationship with Kuwait deteriorated over the former's debts to the latter, and on August 2, Iraq invaded.

International sanctions were immediately applied, and carrier forces from various nations proceeded to the Gulf to enforce them. Interdiction strikes were flown until the war proper started on January 16, 1991, when coalition forces moved in to liberate Kuwait. Air bases were available in Saudi Arabia, but again, the speed and flexibility with which carriers could be dispatched to trouble spots enabled the USN to have a fully functioning air operation present almost immediately.

BELOW: Dassault Super Étendard of the Aéronavale on the catapult of the carrier *Foch*, from where combat missions were flown to hit Hezbollah targets during the Lebanese Civil War in 1983.
Author's collection

HAWKER SIDDELEY SEA HARRIER

Almost nobody expected the VTOL Harrier to make a competitive fighter, capable of going toe-to-toe with conventional combat jets. But the brilliance of the design and the belief of the 'Harrier Mafia' turned the Sea Harrier into one of the most successful carrier aircraft of the jet age.

RIGHT: XS457 of 899 Squadron, the most successful Sea Harrier in air combat, with two aircraft confirmed destroyed, one probably destroyed, and one damaged.
Pete West/ Key Publishing

RIGHT: Three Sea Harrier FRS1s in flight in 1981, the year before deployment to the Falklands, representing the three frontline squadrons operating the type – nearest the camera 899 Squadron, in the middle 800 Squadron, and furthest, 801 Squadron.
Author's collection

BELOW: Sea Harrier FRS1 of 899 Squadron at the Sea Harrier's home base, RNAS Yeovilton, in August 1981 – on the ground, rocket pods and 1,000lb bombs, on the outer pylons, AIM-9 Sidewinder missiles. On May 16, 1982, this aircraft bombed the Argentine supply vessel *Rio Carcarañá*, causing fatal damage.
Ray Thompson

The development of a new class of 'command ship' for the Royal Navy in the 1970s created the space for what became the Sea Harrier. In turn, the Sea Harrier made such a mark that the light, VTOL carrier has since been known colloquially as the 'Harrier Carrier'. Even when the nascent Sea Harrier was conceived though, few had any idea what it would be capable of.

The RN's Invincible-class was conceived as a helicopter carrier mostly focussed on anti-submarine warfare, but the RN included the ability to "Deploy a quick-reaction contribution to limited air defence, probe and strike capability with V/STOL aircraft."

'Limited air defence' meant dealing with enemy reconnaissance aircraft, which could direct bombers, submarines, and stand-off missiles towards the fleet. The RN did not anticipate that the aircraft would be able to deal with conventional combat jets, but that was not the main threat – or so it was believed.

In 1972, the RN requested a 'maritime V/STOL aircraft' based on the Harrier GR1. It was intended for reconnaissance of surface vessels; countering enemy air reconnaissance, control and missile-launching aircraft; and attacking enemy warships. Development began in 1973, with an order for three prototypes and 31 production aircraft following two years later.

One of the more significant differences between the new Sea Harrier and the RAF Harriers that it was based on was air-interception radar. Ferranti was contracted to develop a small, lightweight radar called Blue Fox, developed from a set called Sea Spray that had been created for the Lynx helicopter. The Harrier's nose needed to be lengthened to accommodate it and, as a redesign of the nose was necessary, Hawker Siddeley took the opportunity to move the cockpit up and back, improving visibility for the pilot in all directions. Specialised naval navigation and attack systems were also added, suitable for operation in the shipboard environment.

The Sea Harrier also gained more powerful 'puffer' jets for control in the hover, reflecting the greater turbulence experienced in

SEA HARRIER DATA

FRS1

Length	14.50m (44ft 7in)
Span	7.69m (25ft 3in)
Height	3.71m (12ft 2in)
Empty weight	5,942kg (13,100lb)
Maximum weight	11,884kg (26,200lb)
Maximum speed	740mph
Range (with drop tanks)	3,220km (2,000 miles)
Engine	One × Rolls-Royce Pegasus 104, 20,500lb thrust
Armament	Up to 8,000lb; Air–air missile, AIM-9L/9M Sidewinder, Air–surface missile, BAe Sea Eagle, targeting pod, Matra rocket pods with 18 × 68mm rockets, variety of unguided or laser guided bombs, two × 30mm Aden gun pod.

FA2

As FRS1 unless otherwise specified

Length	14.86m (48ft 9in)
Span	8.10m (26ft 7in)
Empty weight	6,320kg (13,933lb)
Maximum weight	11,880kg (26,190lb)
Engine	One × Rolls-Royce Pegasus 106, 21,500lb thrust
Armament	As FRS1, plus; Air–air missile, four × AIM-120 AMRAAM

SEA HARRIER TIMELINE

First flight – August 20, 1978

First carrier landing, HMS *Hermes* – November 14, 1978

Aircraft delivered to the Royal Navy – June 18, 1979

First front-line Sea Harrier squadron forms (800) – March 31, 1980

First carrier deployment (HMS *Invincible*) – May 20, 1980

Departure for Falklands – April 5, 1982

First combat sortie – May 1, 1982

First air combat victory – May 1, 1982

Assigned to UN forces, Bosnia – April 1993

First FA2 combat sortie – September 8, 1994

Withdrawn from service – March 29, 2006

sea operations, and the airframe and engine made extensive use of corrosion-resistant materials to withstand the harsh sea environment.

In addition to the gun pods, rockets and bombs that could be carried by the RAF Harriers, the Sea Harrier was armed with the AIM-9 Sidewinder missile for air combat, and the Sea Eagle missile for the attack role. The first Sea Harrier FRS1 (for Fighter, Reconnaissance, Strike) flew in August 1978.

Into Service, and Combat

The Fleet Air Arm (FAA) formed a development and trials unit, 700A Squadron, in June 1979 when production aircraft became available, and set about learning about the new aircraft. The first frontline units, 899 and 800 Squadrons, were formed in March 1980 – 899 was to be a land-based headquarters unit, and 800 was assigned to HMS *Invincible*'s air group, later switching to HMS *Hermes*. Its place aboard the new carrier was taken by 801 Squadron, which formed in January 1981.

The Sea Harrier was still extremely new in FAA service, and still in its working up phase, when Argentina invaded the UK territory of the Falkland Islands in April 1982. Three squadrons operated Sea Harriers in that conflict, 800, 801, and 809.

Over the Falklands, the Sea Harrier FRS1 proved, despite being subsonic, that it was able to intercept and destroy aircraft of supersonic capability such as the IAI Dagger, as well as subsonic attack aircraft like the A-4 Skyraider. Sea Harriers were responsible for 23 Argentine aircraft losses, and none were shot down in air combat, though six were lost in accidents or shot down by ground fire. Sea Harriers also damaged several ships and carried out numerous ground attack sorties.

After the Falklands, the Indian Navy bought six Sea Harrier FRS51s (the export version of the FRS1) to operate from the carrier *Vikrant*, which was now too small for conventional jet operations.

The FAA's Sea Harriers underwent various upgrades and improvements in the 1980s–90s and flew over Bosnia during the civil war in 1993–4 from carriers in the Adriatic. Lessons from the Falklands were incorporated into an improved version, the FA2 of 1993, which had a more powerful engine and significantly more capable Blue Vixen radar, plus the ability to carry medium-range AIM-120 AMRAAM missiles, making the FA2 much more potent. The Sea Harrier was retired in 2006.

BELOW LEFT AND BELOW RIGHT: Sea Harrier FA2 ZH801 of 801 Squadron at RNAS Yeovilton, demonstrating the longer and bulkier nose to accommodate the Blue Vixen radar.
Matthew Willis

VERTICAL TAKE-OFF AND LANDING AT SEA

The ability to take off and land from a ship without the complex catapults and arrester gear of conventional carriers proved attractive to several navies from the 1960s, despite criticism of 'jump jet' range, payload, and safety.

RIGHT: Fairey VTO model demonstrating vertical take-off at the Woomera Rocket Range in Australia, 1953.
Author's collection

In the jet age there were two main waves of interest in vertical take-off aircraft that could operate from ships at sea. The first of these came in the late 1940s–early 1950s, and the second in the late 1960s–early 1970s. Ultimately, the first wave came to nothing. The second, however, resulted in fixed-wing Vertical Take-Off and Landing (VTOL) aircraft becoming an established part of carrier aviation.

In fact, it is rare in practice for aircraft to both take off and land vertically, though the aircraft remain capable of it. For this reason, the abbreviation VTOL has typically been superseded by alternatives such as V/STOL (Vertical/Short Take-Off and Landing) or STOVL (Short Take-Off and Vertical Landing). For convenience, VTOL will generally be used below.

Carrier navies first became interested in VTOL due to fears that the aircraft carrier in its current form was doomed. From the late 1940s, the increasing size, cost and importance of carriers made the prospect of their destruction ever more serious. And with the arrival of guided anti-ship missiles and nuclear weapons, the prospect of their destruction seemed ever more likely. At the same time, there seemed to be a genuine possibility that before long, conventional aircraft would not be able to operate from carriers.

The concurrent arrival of the jet engine seemed to offer both a respite for the carrier and an alternative to it. Jet thrust offered a means of taking off vertically, and possibly even landing too, if it could be controlled.

In 1946, the British Fairey Aviation Company began working on a concept for use on ships. The Fairey VTO was a series of turbojet-powered 'tail sitting' designs, beginning with swept wings but later a delta planform, together with the necessary infrastructure to operate them.

Launching was the easy part – to land, the Fairey was required to hover, standing on its tail with the cockpit swivelling to remain level, and manoeuvre into a net.

The challenges involved in keeping aircraft stable and under control under these circumstances were formidable. Nevertheless, the government supported Fairey to test scale models of the aircraft and its launching apparatus, and two full-sized prototypes were ordered, as the Fairey Delta. By the time it flew, in 1951, the idea of a VTOL interceptor had lost appeal, and the Ministry was chiefly interested in it for research into its delta wing. The Delta only ever flew conventionally, and the second prototype was not completed.

In 1947, on the other side of the Atlantic, Ryan Aeronautical independently arrived at a similar concept. The US Navy awarded the company a contract to develop a technology demonstrator for a fighter that could launch from small ships and even submarines.

The Ryan design was, like the Fairey VTO, a small, single-engined delta. The company built a test rig powered by an Allison J33 and carried out trials that enabled it to develop a control system with a mix of jet exhaust deflection and hot air discharge. It was able to hover while tethered in October 1950, and freely just over a year later. After the Korean War, however, the USN's budget was cut dramatically, and the VTOL project was a casualty.

The same year that the Ryan project began, the US Navy initiated Project Hummingbird, for a tail-sitting turboprop fighter that could be launched from an auxiliary ship or temporary coastal base. Convair and Lockheed were commissioned to build prototypes, the XFY-1 and XFV-1, respectively. The Lockheed project was a low priority at the company, which had lost faith in the VTOL concept, and it never made a vertical take-off. Convair's aircraft, nicknamed the 'Pogo' did make several vertical take-offs, and successfully transitioned to horizontal flight, but the difficulties with control, especially during vertical landing, were abundant, and the USN cancelled the project in 1956.

From Land Back to Sea

In the 1960s, NATO air forces took a strong interest in VTOL developments. The Korean War highlighted the difficulty of providing air support to ground operations with few available airbases. Then, as the nuclear arms race gathered pace, fears grew that a nuclear first strike by the USSR would destroy the majority of airbases across Europe and »

BELOW: US Marine Corps AV-8A Harrier of VMA-513 hovering over the deck of USS *Guam* during trials in 1972, while a US Navy Sikorsky SH-3A hovers aft. Author's collection

render NATO unable to resist an invasion. NATO Basic Requirement 3 (NBMR-3) was issued in June 1961 for a VTOL supersonic interceptor and strike fighter that could operate from unprepared sites, as well as other VTOL aircraft such as a subsonic ground attack aircraft.

Manufacturers from the UK, France, Germany, the Netherlands, USA, and Italy submitted designs, and the technical winner was the British Hawker Siddeley P.1154. At the same time, the Royal Navy was starting to consider a replacement for the Fleet Air Arm's (FAA) de Havilland Sea Vixen all-weather fighter, and the Ministry of Defence suggested that the P.1154 could be adapted to meet FAA needs.

NBMR-3 was dead by the mid-1960s as the contributing nations were unable to agree on which aircraft to acquire, and although the UK government had intended to procure the P.1154 for both the RAF and the FAA regardless of the NATO decision, a change of government in 1964 led to the programme being scrapped. The idea of carrier capable VTOL jets, though, would not die with the P.1154.

Toe In The Water

Since the late 1950s, Hawker Siddeley and Bristol had collaborated on the development of a VTOL strike fighter. Bristol developed the Pegasus, a turbofan engine with swivelling nozzles to provide 'thrust vectoring' – in other words, steering the jet exhaust to provide thrust for hovering or normal flight from the same engine. Hawker designed the P.1127 around this engine, essentially as a private venture.

There was considerable interest in the project from NATO and the US, both of which provided development funding. In October 1960, tethered hovering tests took place and the following month the UK government requested a further four prototypes.

The first prototype was hovering in November 1960, flying conventionally

in February 1961, and transitioned from vertical to horizontal flight in May. NMBR-3's requirements were far too ambitious for the P.1127 to meet, and although there was much attention on the aircraft, it was regarded chiefly as a development tool for much more capable types to come.

The P.1127's relative simplicity, however, which had been insisted upon by Hawker Siddeley chief designer Sydney Camm, played in its favour when technical and political problems beset the NATO competition.

Although the chief interest in VTOL was land-based, there was by now a realisation that VTOL jets could operate from aircraft carriers, or indeed, virtually any ship that a helicopter could operate from.

In February 1963, test pilot Bill Bedford made the first VTOL deck

landing aboard an aircraft carrier, HMS *Ark Royal*, in prototype P.1127 XP381. He went on to make a further 11 take-offs and landings, half the take-offs vertical, half conventional.

A pre-production version known as the Kestrel was trialled by the US Navy and Marine Corps in 1966, including landings aboard the carrier USS *Independence* and the amphibious landing ship USS *Raleigh*. The Royal Navy conducted similar trials aboard HMS *Bulwark*.

Finally, the aircraft was ordered into production as the Harrier, partly as a compensation to the RAF for the cancellation of the P.1154. Initially the British version would be strictly for the RAF, though in 1969 Navy Minister David Owen raised the possibility of RAF Harriers operating from RN commando carriers.

Hawker Siddeley was keen to demonstrate the possibilities offered

ABOVE, BELOW AND OPPOSITE: US Marine Corps AV-8A Harriers operating from an amphibious assault ship. Author's collection

by shipboard VTOL. In the late 1960s–early 1970s, John Farley, chief test pilot for the Harrier programme, undertook a series of trial landings aboard aircraft carriers and other warships with flight decks. In 1969, he landed on the relatively small deck on the stern of the amphibious transport USS *La Salle*.

In February 1973, Farley landed a Harrier on the stern deck of the helicopter cruiser *Jeanne d'Arc*, and on November 14–15, made several landings aboard the carrier *Foch* in the Bay of Biscay as part of preparations for possible French adoption of the new aircraft. In the early 1970s, the Marine Nationale

developed the 'Blue Plan' to renew its carrier forces, with four new nuclear-powered vessels – two strike carriers and two commando assault vessels. The latter, in addition to 15–25 helicopters, could operate VTOL jets in the close support role.

Farley asked *Foch*'s captain to make his job as difficult as possible, though the typically rough conditions in those waters were challenging enough. Farley landed on the yawing, pitching, water-slicked deck successfully, though during one particularly large roll, the Harrier almost slid overboard.

The Marine Nationale did not proceed with the idea of VTOL close support jets, but the trials led to an unconventional idea that attracted significant attention at

Hawker Siddeley into the 1980s. The 'SkyHook' concept, patented in 1982, was brainstormed by Hawker Siddeley designer John Fozard and test pilot Heinz Frick, as a response to the continuing risk of aircraft sliding off the deck.

The resulting 'Skyhook' concept proposed that instead of landing, the aircraft hovered beside the ship. The aircraft would engage with a stabilised 'hook' suspended from a boom, to be safely swung on board when secure. Trial versions of the hardware were built, and the viability of the scheme demonstrated. Several navies expressed interest, but none made the leap.

One service that did see the possibilities offered by the Harrier, however, was the US Marine Corps. »

Harrier Vs Yak-38

The Yak-38 has often been criticised in the West, not least for its three-engined configuration, with two lift engines effectively dead weight in normal flight. How did the only two VTOL jets to see service in the 20th century stack up against each other?

The Yak-38 could count on 28,750lb of thrust from its three engines, compared with 20,500lb from the Pegasus 103 in the contemporary Harrier GR3. The Rybinsk lift engines together added 402kg (886lb) to the overall weight, and while a reliable figure is not available for the weight of the R-28V-300, the preceding R-27V-300 had a dry weight of 1,350kg (2,976lb) for a combined total of 1,752kg (3,862lb). The Pegasus 103 weighed 1,642kg (3,619lb), so even allowing for weight increases in the later engine, the Yak's arrangement appears competitive with that of the Harrier in terms of thrust Vs weight.

Of course, only 15,300lb thrust from the main engine was available to the Yak-38 in forward flight, but the deficit in thrust was partly compensated for by a reduction in drag due to smaller intakes. The empty weight of the Yak was some 2,745lb greater than that of the Harrier while its maximum take-off weight was only 815lb greater, so the difference in useful payload is all too apparent. The Yak-38M was a significant improvement, but by the time of its introduction in 1985, the US and UK had moved on to the Harrier II, which had moved the goalposts considerably in terms of performance and utility.

The Yak's load-carrying ability and range were relatively poor, but its superb all-axis stabilisation and well-integrated controls in VTOL flight meant it was capable of operating from smaller ship platforms than the Harrier, and in worse weather. It was also safer for pilots in the event of a failure with its automatic escape system.

The Yak's small wing gave it good dash speed, but according to USMC pilot Art Nalls, who flew a Yak-38 after the Cold War: "Manoeuvring performance was only adequate and wingborne handling qualities leave a lot to be desired."

The AV-8ors

Ships could take VTOL jets anywhere in the world for them to operate either from the ship itself or ashore. The idea promised to restore a capability to the USMC which it had lost when jets superseded propeller aircraft. During World War Two and Korea, the USMC had operated aircraft from escort carriers based on merchant ship hulls in support of amphibious operations. The escort carriers, small and cheap, could be operated close inshore where large carriers could not. VTOL offered a way to put close-support jets aboard USMC helicopter carriers. USMC Major Woody Gilliland wrote in 1978 that: "The Harrier offered Marine aviation the speed, firepower and survivability of a jet with the basing flexibility of a helicopter."

In 1968, two years after the service's Kestrel trials, the USMC decided to acquire Harriers, under the designation AV-8A. The first aircraft entered service in 1971. The highly unusual move of a US military service acquiring a foreign type was made necessary by the failure of all domestic efforts to develop a VTOL aircraft to production, though this is to take nothing away from the abilities of the Harrier even in its early form. Maj Gilliland wrote: "The Harrier provided a marked improvement in V/STOL operational effectiveness without an unacceptable degrading of performance characteristics; at the same time, it did not require a great increase in overall support and maintenance."

The USMC found that VTOL aircraft based ashore usefully reduced the time it took to answer calls for close support, as the aircraft could be based close to the front line, and vertical take-off improved response times.

When based on an amphibious assault or helicopter assault ship, the USMC found that a detachment of six Harriers could operate effectively without any detrimental effects on the ship's helicopter operations. Use of a rolling take-off was possible, dramatically increasing payload, and the ships could readily support extended operations.

A third mode of deployment was on the flight deck of any vessel capable of operating a helicopter. These were essentially used as a forward base, which a Harrier could stage to from its main carrier, closer inshore to await calls for support.

BELOW: The first prototype YAV-8B Harrier, 71-58394, during carrier suitability trials aboard USS *Saipan* from Patuxent River in October 1979. The YAV-8Bs were AV-8A airframes modified with the B-model wing.
Author's collection

LEFT: Sea Harrier FRS1 XZ458 of 800 Squadron flown by Lieutenant Commander R.V. Frederiksen demonstrating hovering flight at Farnborough in 1980. Both Frederiksen and XZ458 flew in the Falklands two years later. The Sea Harrier was delivered aboard the *Atlantic Conveyer* in May and flew 45 sorties with 809 and 801 Squadrons aboard HMS *Invincible*. Frederiksen, with 800 Squadron, destroyed one aircraft on the ground on May 1 and shot down an IAI Dagger on May 21.
Ray Thompson

The USMC even operated Harriers from a fleet carrier, USS *Franklin D Roosevelt*, in 1976, proving that the type could operate in weather that would ground conventional carrier aircraft.

There was a down side. The Harrier was difficult to fly, especially in VTOL flight. Between 1971 and 1978, 27 of the USMC's 110 AV-8As crashed, with the loss of 11 pilots. Critics also pointed out that the AV-8A could only carry half the payload of the A-4 Skyhawk, over a smaller range. Even so, by 1978, the USMC was convinced of the value of VTOL jets and lobbied hard for replacement of the AV-8A with an improved Harrier instead of a conventional jet. As well as the USMC, the Thai Navy bought AV-8As.

Hawker Siddeley and McDonnell Douglas had begun working on what would become the AV-8B in 1973. The aircraft was significantly revised, with wide use of modern composites, a larger wing and tail,

more powerful engine, and much improved avionics. Prototypes were tested in 1978–79, and 336 aircraft ordered for the Marines. Spain and Italy also purchased the type for shipboard operation, as the Harrier made fixed-wing carrier aviation viable for small navies.

USMC AV-8Bs entered squadron service in 1984–85 and saw combat in the Gulf War of 1991, during which over 3,000 flights were made, and five aircraft were shot down by surface-to-air missiles. The Harrier remains in USMC service as of 2024.

Sea Harrier

When the possibility of RAF Harriers operating from Royal Navy carriers was raised in 1969, Hawker Siddeley quickly developed proposals for a bona fide naval version. Though the government had decided that there was no further use for conventional carriers, the RN was developing anti-submarine and command ships with

continuous flight decks that could potentially operate VTOL jets. This would emerge as the Invincible-class ship of around 20,000 tons, three of which were ordered in the early 1970s.

The RN saw the value of a dedicated naval Harrier, for use as a maritime strike platform and as an interceptor. It was not thought that the aircraft could stand against land-based fighters, but as the Soviet Navy had concluded, would be suitable against shadowing reconnaissance aircraft which could direct anti-ship missiles. The naval Harrier would be equipped with radar and short-range air-to-air missiles, though it would also be capable of ground attack.

To help the aircraft take off at a greater weight, a 'ski jump' was developed, with trials on land proving successful, and they were added to all three ships. Most carriers operating VTOL aircraft now use the ski jump. »

BELOW: The second YAV-8B in flight in September 1979 demonstrating the new model's prodigious lifting capacity with eight bombs and two Sidewinder missiles.
Author's collection

In 1975 the Ministry of Defence consented to the FAA acquiring 34 Sea Harrier FRS1 aircraft, the first of which entered service in 1978. The aircraft proved highly effective in the ground attack role during the Falklands conflict of 1982, and, more surprisingly, as a fighter against conventional attack jets such as the A-4 Skyhawk and Dassault Mirage. It was upgraded to FA2 status from 1985, with more powerful engine, more capable radar and AIM-120 AMRAAM missiles which made it a formidable package. The Sea Harrier also saw action over Bosnia and Kosovo in the 1990s and the type was withdrawn in 2006.

VTOL in the USSR

From the late 1940s, the Soviet Navy's leaders held the firm opinion that the aircraft carrier was too vulnerable to submarines and missiles, and of little use in the kind of war that the USSR expected, where a protracted fight for command of the sea was unthinkable. This view began to change in the 1960s, and while there was still resistance to a large, conventional carrier, the value of a ship that could carry a few strike jets began to be recognised.

A ship-based jet could attack targets on the coast anywhere in the world. It could provide additional defence, and even provide a measure of air defence against patrol aircraft.

The Soviet Navy began building the Moskva-class helicopter carriers in the early 1960s. By the late 1960s, the Soviet Navy had even more ambitious

LEFT: Sea Harrier FA2 ZA195 in a vertical climb in January 1989, carrying four AIM-120 AMRAAM missiles.
Author's collection

BELOW: The second prototype Yakovlev Yak-36 'Freehand' at Monino aviation museum in 1993.
Ray Thompson

LEFT: Crowded flight deck of a Kiev-class carrier in the late 1970s, with eight Yak-38s, wings folded for maximum compactness, and a Kamov Ka-25 helicopter. The ceramic tiles on the deck to resist the heat of the jet thrust are apparent. Author's collection

plans for ship-based aviation and the third Moskva-class, *Kiev*, was cancelled and re-ordered as a vastly bigger and more capable ship.

This was chiefly intended to offer a significant increase in anti-submarine capacity, but Soviet naval strategists had been eyeing the possibilities offered by aircraft like the Yak-36 technology demonstrator, which had flown in 1966.

The Yak-36 was fitted with two Tumansky R-27 turbojets in the nose, the jet thrust exiting the lower fuselage beneath the wing, at the centre of gravity. It first underwent tethered hovering tests in June 1963, followed by transitions to level flight in October that year, and full VTOL flight, with a vertical take-off followed by transition to normal flight then a vertical landing, in March 1966.

The Soviet Navy ordered a production aircraft, the Yak-38, in 1973, and it began equipping frontline squadrons in 1975 (see page 84). Some 231 were built, and the type served with three Soviet fleets until the end of the Cold War.

Yakovlev developed a much more capable supersonic VTOL shipboard fighter, the Yak-141, but it was cancelled with the end of the Cold War and the Russian Navy's decision to pursue short take-off but arrested landing (CATOBAR) carriers.

BELOW: The Yakovlev Yak-141 'Freestyle' supersonic VTOL prototype at the Moscow Airshow in 1993. Ray Thompson

YAKOVLEV YAK-38 *FORGER*

The first naval vertical take-off and landing (VTOL) jet was the Yak-38, an innovative if flawed aircraft that took the Soviet Navy into carrier aviation.

RIGHT: Yak-38 '73 Yellow' of the 279 OKShAP, air group *Kiev*, January 1988.
Matthew Willis

RIGHT: Yak-38 '24 Yellow' makes a vertical take-off from the carrier *Kiev* in the Atlantic during trials in August 1976, seen from the RN frigate HMS *Torquay*. The open lift engine doors and downward-angled jet nozzles are seen to good effect.
Author's collection

Designers in the Soviet Union first became interested in VTOL in the 1950s, and after experiments with testbeds, the Yakovlev design bureau began working on the resulting Yak-36 technology demonstrator (NATO reporting name *Freehand*) in 1961. The aircraft achieved VTOL flight by angling the exhaust nozzles down, stability in the hover provided by a system of air jets in the aircraft's extremities.

The Yak-36 proved the viability of the concept, but the VVS (Soviet Air Force) did not pursue it despite the popularity of the VTOL attack jet concept in the 1960s. The Soviet Navy, on the other hand, developed an interest as the large, powerful anti-submarine cruisers of the Kiev-class took shape.

In 1967, Yakovlev was commissioned to develop an operational aircraft based on Yak-36 experience. On the earlier aircraft, thrust-vectoring of the main engines alone provided insufficient thrust to enable VTOL operation with a worthwhile payload, and a different approach was sought.

The new aircraft was designated Yak-36M, despite being a completely fresh design. In contrast to the dumpy

BELOW: US Navy photograph of Yak-38 '14 Yellow' approaching *Kiev* from astern to make a landing during trials in the Atlantic in August 1976.
Author's collection

Yak-36, it was a long, slim aircraft, with small, mid-mounted delta wings. The Tumansky R-27-V300 main engine had a bifurcated jetpipe with swivelling nozzles to either side, low on the rear fuselage. Two Rybinsk RD-36-35FV lightweight engines were positioned in tandem behind the cockpit, aligned almost vertically to provide lift during take-off and landing. At all other times they would be shut down, dead weight in normal flight, but the arrangement provided more thrust than any single engine then available and was in some respects simpler than the alternatives.

The prototype VM-01 was completed in 1970 and was tested in the spring of that year by Yakovlev test pilot Mikhail Sergeyevich Deksbakh.

Trials with the helicopter cruiser *Moskva* saw Deksbakh make the first deck landing on November 18, 1972. Assessment flights with the ship travelling at different speeds, in a range of weather conditions and sea states, proved that the Yak was eminently suitable for shipboard operations. An order was consequently placed for a production version designated Yak-38.

In Service

In a rare example of inter-service co-operation, the Soviet Air Force (VVS) undertook the development programme for the Yak-38. Many complex problems had to be addressed, in particular the flight control system for VTOL flight. This involved integrating operation of the engine and flight control systems to maintain stability while responding predictably to control inputs. The pilot controlled the aircraft in the hover with a single throttle lever that operated all three engines, with thrust vector control via a switch on the main stick.

The control system was highly effective. US test pilot Art Nalls, who flew Harriers with the Marine Corps, wrote: "It is remarkable that this fully integrated flight and propulsion system was developed in the early 70s and operational in 1975." He added: "The handling qualities of the Yak-38U in VSTOL flight are excellent," with "low workload" and "high precision."

A special escape system was developed for the Yak as in VTOL flight, a failure could occur too quickly for the pilot to react.

YAK-38 DATA	
Length	16.4m (53ft 8in)
Span	7.17.1m (23ft 3in)
Height	4.25m (13ft 11in)
Empty weight	7,385kg (16,280lb)
Maximum weight	11,800kg (26,015lb)
Maximum speed	715mph
Range (internal fuel)	600km (375 miles)
Engine	One × Tumansky R-28-300, 13,500lb thrust, two × Rybinsk RD-36-35FV 5,000lb thrust
Armament	Up to 2,000kg; Air–air missile, Molniya R-60 (NATO AA-8 *Aphid*), Air–surface missile, Kh-23 Grom (NATO AS-7 *Kerry*)/ C-24B rocket , targeting pod, rocket pod four × UB16 or two × UB32, bomb two × 100kg or 250kg, UPK-23 gun pod.

Yak-38M	
As Yak-38 unless otherwise specified	
Maximum weight	12,000kg (26,455lb)
Range	680km (420 miles)
Engine	One × Tumansky R-28-300, 15,000lb thrust, two × Rybinsk RD-38, 7,000lb thrust
Armament	As Yak-38, plus two × 500kg/four × 250kg bomb

YAK-38 TIMELINE
First flight (Yak-36M) – January 15, 1971
First VTOL flight (Yak-36M) – May 25, 1971
First deck landing – November 18, 1972
First carrier deployment, *Kiev* – July 1976
Formal service entry – October 1976
First Pacific Fleet deployment – April 1979
First combat deployment (Afghanistan) – April 1980
First interception while carrying missiles – December 16, 1982
Cargo ship trials – September 1983
Introduction of Yak-38M – June 1985
Withdrawal from service – December 1991

the Black Sea the following year. The Yak-38 was officially admitted into frontline service in October.

The second Kiev-class ship, *Minsk*, commissioned in 1978, and took part in an exercise with her sister in the Mediterranean, involving five Yak-38s from each vessel. The third vessel, *Novorossiysk*, commissioned in 1982, and mainly served in the Pacific.

Operational evaluation in Afghanistan proved the unsuitability of the Yak-38 for operation in hot and high settings. High temperatures severely dented the aircraft's usefulness at sea, too, with already small payloads and range impacted. However, experiments operating from platforms on cargo ships were more successful. Throughout the Yak-38's career, continued experience helped develop hardware and procedures, bringing steady improvements in performance and capability. This increased further with the introduction of the refined Yak-38M, which featured more powerful engines. The type served with the 279th, 299th and 311th Regiments in the Northern, Black Sea, and Pacific Fleets. On numerous occasions the Yak made successful interceptions of, on-paper, higher performing US Navy aircraft, and shepherded them away from Soviet naval forces.

The Yak-38 saw out the Cold War but was retired in the early 1990s when the Russian Navy switched to more conventional carriers. A total of 231 production Yak-38s were built including 50 Yak-38M and 38 Yak-38U.

ABOVE: Yak-38 No. 7977863822385, the fourth aircraft of the seventh production batch, 'Yellow 46', built 1979, aboard the carrier *Minsk* in the South China Sea in November 1982, photographed from a US Navy aircraft. Author's collection

BELOW: Late standard Yak-38 '60 Yellow' at Khodynka, Moscow, in 1993, demonstrating the dorsal strakes (to prevent exhaust ingestion) and larger tail cone added to aircraft during maintenance cycles, and four UB32 rocket pods. Ray Thompson

Professor G. I. Severin developed an automated version of his K-36 ejection seat which reacted to developing problems faster than a human could.

The Yak-38 lacked modern features such as a head-up display, however, with only a basic ranging radar plus an infra-red sensor. Its suite of weapons included rocket pods, 'dumb' bombs, gun packs, and short-range air-to-air and air-to-ground missiles.

The chief complaints about the Yak-38 were poor endurance and a high failure rate in components such as the lift engines. The development of rolling take-off and landings, however, reduced the heavy fuel use in VTOL to an extent, while auxiliary tanks increased range. The automated escape system saved numerous lives when failures occurred – once pilots learned to trust it and consented to enable it.

A two-seat version, the Yak-38U, was developed for conversion training.

The 279 OKShAP (Independent Shipboard Attack Air Regiment) began working up with Yak-36M pre-production aircraft in 1973. Production Yak-38s began equipping Soviet Naval Aviation in 1975, and the aircraft first came to the attention of the West when it embarked aboard *Kiev* during a preparatory cruise in

THE HELICOPTER AND THE CARRIER

At the beginning of the jet age, aircraft carriers were designed around fixed-wing aircraft, and their rotary-wing counterparts played only a minor role. As the technology matured, particularly thanks to the turboshaft engine, helicopters increasingly supplanted aeroplanes.

The helicopter is synonymous with the jet age, particularly in naval aviation, even though the early machines were themselves piston-engined. The first naval helicopters proved their worth during the Korean War. They vastly increased safety in flying operations by replacing both fixed-wing air-sea rescue amphibians and the 'plane guard' ship – a vessel that traditionally operated with a carrier to pick up aircrews who crashed into the sea during take-off or landing.

The helicopter was faster to respond than both a fixed-wing seaplane and the plane-guard ship, which had to launch a boat to pick up downed crewmen. It was also safer for all concerned. The positioning of a plane-guard ship was critical during flying operations and there was a significant risk of collision. The Royal Australian Navy carrier HMAS *Melbourne* was involved in serious collisions with two plane-guard destroyers, in both cases slicing the smaller ship in two with some loss of life. The helicopter did not completely supplant the plane-guard

ship, but it did significantly reduce its use, especially during the daytime.

When jets first started routinely operating from US Navy (USN) carriers in the late 1940s, it was apparent that their characteristics made the need for prompt and precise rescue even more apparent. The unreliable early jets could 'flame out' on take-off, and the lack of a propeller made barriers less effective on landing. The increased speed at which everything took place magnified errors.

The first rescue of a ditched carrier aircraft crew took place on February 9, 1947, when a Sikorsky S-51 picked up Lieutenant Robert Shields after an engine failure had forced him to put his aircraft down on the water. The aviator was back on the deck of USS *Franklin D Roosevelt* no more than six or seven minutes after announcing that he needed to ditch. The S-51 was piloted by Sikorsky test pilot Jimmy Viner, who was flying the machine with Task Fleet 2 as a trial and demonstration of the helicopter's value. It was proved in no uncertain terms that day and the rest of the exercises only confirmed the

point. The USN purchased 48 S-51s, designated Ho3S (later H-5).

The helicopter represented such a sea-change in rescue operations that the USN lent helicopters and crews to Royal Navy carriers operating off Korea.

Moreover, the ability of the helicopter to operate over land as well as water, and land virtually anywhere, gave the USN the ability to rescue aircrews downed over land as well, even behind enemy lines, a possibility which had barely existed for preceding fixed-wing aircraft. This facility was used to great effect in Korea, though the performance of early helicopters placed limits on what was possible.

The characteristics that made helicopters capable of retrieving personnel from the shore and returning them to a carrier also made them able to deliver personnel ashore. The US Marine Corps (USMC) quickly realised the possibilities offered for amphibious assault and began to develop this capability before the 1940s were out.

Korea threw up numerous roles in naval warfare that the helicopter

BELOW:
Supermarine
Scimitar of 800
Squadron, Fleet
Air Arm – a rather
accident-prone
type – readies
to launch from
HMS *Ark Royal* in
the early 1960s,
while the plane-
guard Westland
Whirlwind
maintains a very
close watch.
Author's collection

was perfect for that had not even been dreamt of when they were first developed. During the Wosnan landings in October 1950, an HO3S was used to spot submerged sea mines, leading to minesweeping teams being allocated helicopters permanently, along with support facilities.

Anti-submarine warfare

It was the anti-submarine role that turned the helicopter from a useful but niche part of an air group to a major part of it, equal if not greater in importance than the fixed-wing aircraft.

As FAA pilot Lieutenant Commander Ian Sloan put it: "Anti-submarine warfare in 1940 was three guys, one torpedo, 90 knots. In 1990 it was three guys, one torpedo, 90 knots." Low speed and loiter was an important factor in anti-submarine aircraft, which became increasingly specialised throughout World War Two and after. As soon as helicopters were capable of carrying a reasonable load, it was a natural development to explore how they could contribute to anti-submarine warfare.

During World War Two, sonobuoys were developed, which could be dropped into the sea where they responded to acoustic signals and transmitted information to the aircraft above. The helicopter's ability to hover meant that it could directly lower an active sonar unit into the water with a direct link to the aircraft, the so-called 'dipping sonar'. Active sonar had to be used very sparingly by ships as it could be homed in on by a submarine. A helicopter, however, was at far less risk. When initial engineering

problems were overcome, helicopters were found to be extremely complementary with fixed-wing anti-submarine aircraft, and mixed units of helicopters and Grumman Trackers were carried on US carriers. The RN's Fleet Air Arm (FAA) started introducing Westland Whirlwinds in the anti-submarine role in 1953, although the piston-engined versions of this model could not carry both dipping sonar and a torpedo at the same time, so pairs of aircraft operated on anti-submarine patrol.

So concerned was the USN about the risk of Soviet attack submarines interfering with carrier operations around the world that from the mid-1950s it began to configure older carriers as ASW carriers, alongside the main attack carriers. Specialist ASW carriers had been in USN service since 1950, but the adoption of Essex-class fleet carriers in the »

role brought about a huge increase in capability. These ships had an air group of S-2 Trackers and Sikorsky HSS Choctaw helicopters.

The USN maintained a fixed-wing anti-submarine capability, introducing the Lockheed S-3 Viking in 1974 to replace the Tracker. The FAA, however, went all-helicopter in the ASW role in 1960 with the retirement of the Fairey Gannet AS1/4 aircraft. Other navies, such as the Royal Canadian Navy, significantly increased the proportion of ASW rotorcraft in their air groups from the early 1960s, in some cases phasing out combat aircraft altogether.

The Soviet Union approached the problem from the other direction. The Military Maritime Fleet of the USSR largely rejected aircraft carriers as white elephants until the mid-1950s, but the USN's development of submarine launched intercontinental ballistic missiles pushed the development of ASW forces.

Two ASW helicopter carriers were laid down in the early 1960s. Reflecting the Soviet ambivalence about carriers, the Moskva-class helicopter carriers incorporated many of the features of missile cruisers as well as accommodating 12 Kamov Ka-25 (NATO reporting name *Hormone*) anti-submarine helicopters. The Ka-25 was initiated in 1958, and first flew in 1963. It reflected several points of divergence from typical Western designs. N.I. Kamov ploughed a solitary furrow in developing helicopters with contra-rotating rotors on a single axis. This made the helicopter compact, as the tail rotor was not required, which was useful for shipboard operation.

The Ka-25 was equipped with dipping sonar and two homing torpedoes, as well as search radar in a prominent chin radome. It operated from cruisers as well as the Moskva-class ships, and then the much larger Kiev-class introduced in the 1970s (see VTOL chapter).

The Jet Age catches up

While the majority of significant advances in helicopter technology in the early part of the jet era came from the US, one of the biggest improvements had its origins in the UK – gas turbine powerplants. Westland Aircraft (later Westland Helicopters) was an 'early adopter' of rotary wing technology and entered into a licencing agreement with the American Sikorsky company in 1948. Westland started building versions of Sikorsky designs tailored to British requirements, with the Westland Dragonfly an adaptation of the S-51, followed in 1950 by the Whirlwind, a development of the S-55 Chickasaw. In 1955, Westland prepared for production of a licence-built version of the S-58, in USN service as the H-34 Choctaw, which it named Wessex.

The Choctaw was, as with most US military helicopters at the time, powered by an air-cooled radial piston engine. This gave good

ABOVE: HMS Ark Royal, escorted by eight Westland Wessex helicopters, arrives at Devonport at the beginning of her 1961–63 commission, demonstrating how important a part of a carrier's air group helicopters were becoming. Author's collection

reliability, as the engines typically used such as the Choctaw's Wright R-1820, were extremely mature designs. Westland, however, took the step of re-engineering the Choctaw to take its power from a Napier Gazelle gas turbine.

A jet engine can be configured to drive a propeller or a shaft (hence the terms 'turboprop' and 'turboshaft') to generate energy, rather than directing its power to thrust alone. Turbomeca in France was the first company to develop a turboshaft for rotary wing aircraft, adapting an aeroplane's auxiliary power unit, while the first helicopter to be fitted with the new style powerplant was an experimental Kamen twin-rotor aircraft in the US in 1951. However, it was Westland that first introduced the turboshaft as a standard powerplant on a production naval helicopter.

A big attraction in switching rotorcraft from piston engines to turbine power was logistical. In the 1950s as it switched from propeller to jet aeroplanes, the Royal Navy was keen to eradicate Avgas (petrol) from its carriers, due to the fire risk and the impracticality of maintaining storage and supply systems for two different kinds of fuel.

The Gazelle brought additional advantages, however. Although it was slightly less powerful than the Wright

R-1820 used in the Choctaw, and burned more fuel, it was significantly lighter, overall improving the aircraft's power-to-weight ratio. Unlike the Whirlwind, the Wessex could carry both dipping sonar and two homing torpedoes, so could now operate individually.

The turbine also reduced vibration compared with the piston engine, which brought benefits in anti-submarine operations and medical evacuation. The turbine could also be started up far more quickly, improving response and turnaround times, especially in cold weather.

The Gazelle-powered Wessex helicopters were such a success that the RN rebuilt a number of its existing piston-engined Whirlwind helicopters with de Havilland Gnome turboshaft power.

The US Navy followed suit when the SH-3 Sea King entered service in 1961, proving that the turboshaft allowed significant increases in performance, reliability, and capability.

Going Commando

The utility of the helicopter for amphibious assault led to a specialist type of aircraft carrier being developed to exploit this, colloquially known as the 'commando carrier'. However, they are often considered a different class of vessel to aircraft

carriers. This has its origin in the USN deliberately classifying its commando carriers with amphibious landing ships rather than with carriers for funding purposes. The original USN commando carrier, USS *Thetis*, was classified CVHA, for Carrier Vehicle Helicopter Assault, in 1956 but reclassified LPH (Landing Platform Helicopter) three years later.

As with the ASW carrier, successive commando carriers tended to be bigger and more capable than their predecessors, and former attack carriers were converted to this role too.

The British experience was initially more ad hoc. The RN hurriedly converted two Colossus-class light fleet carriers, HMS *Ocean,* and HMS *Theseus* into commando carrier status ahead of anticipated military action over the Suez Crisis (see End Of Empire). In fact, these two ships had just been converted into troop ships, so the work involved a certain amount of 're-conversion' to allow them to operate aircraft again. The anti-submarine Whirlwinds of 845 Squadron were re-tasked to fly Royal Marines onto the shore, this becoming the first ever combat amphibious assault by helicopter in history.

The Crisis erupted into combat on October 29, 1956, though *Ocean* »

ABOVE: A Royal Navy 'Junglie' commando Sea King HC4 ZF115 of 848 Squadron in Arctic camouflage during celebrations of the 40th anniversary of the Sea King's RN service.
Matthew Willis

and *Theseus* did not leave Malta until November 3. The Whirlwinds were stripped of any nonessential equipment to help fit as many Marines as possible on board – the FAA aircraft could take seven fully equipped Marine Commandos compared with five for the RAF equivalent.

On November 6, the helicopters took off from HMS *Ocean* and

Theseus and carried their troops to Port Saïd, landing 415 Marines and 23 tons of ammunition and equipment in just under an hour and a half.

Militarily, the campaign was plagued by indecision and muddle, and politically it was a disaster, but the first ever commando assault by helicopter from a carrier was in itself a conspicuous success. Thereafter, the Royal Navy operated a dedicated

force of commando helicopters, known as 'Junglies', starting with the Whirlwind, switching to the Wessex when the larger machine became available and, in 1969, the still larger Sea King.

The lessons of Suez were also not lost on the USN. In 1971, construction began on USS *Tarawa*, the first of a class of five ships which combined the functions of several different

ABOVE: Sikorsky HH-60H Rescue Hawk #155117 on the deck of USS *Constellation* in 1996. The Rescue Hawk is a search and rescue, and special operations variant of the SH-60 Sea Hawk, which was introduced in 1984 to replace the SH-2 Seasprite. This aircraft was lost with all crew off Coronado Island in 2009 while operating from USS *Nimitz*.
Ray Thompson

LEFT: A Kamov Ka-25 (NATA name *Hormone*) anti-submarine helicopter of the Military Maritime Fleet of the USSR at Monino in 1993.
Ray Thompson

previous classes of amphibious assault ship into one vessel. *Tarawa* and her sisters could operate large helicopters such as the twin-rotor CH-46 Sea Knight and single rotor CH-53 Sea Stallion. They could also operate VTOL jets and landing craft.

Early Warning

When the FAA retired its last conventional carrier, HMS *Ark Royal*, in 1978, the Fairey Gannet AEW3, and the RN's airborne early warning capability, went with it. This proved a to be a very serious problem in the Falklands conflict of 1982 when attacks by Argentine Navy and Air Force jets at very low level, using the islands as cover, confounded the ship-based radar. AEW for the fleet was supposed to be provided by the RAF's ageing Avro Shackletons, but they lacked the range to support the RN's operations in the South Atlantic.

The loss of HMS *Sheffield* on May 4, 1982, to an air-launched Exocet anti-ship missile, brought the lack of AEW home in no uncertain terms. The RN and the Directorate of Naval Air Warfare at the Ministry of Defence began to consider options to restore the capability quickly. Fortunately, Thorn EMI had already done some work on fitting a new airborne search radar into a Sea King helicopter. The company's Searchwater radar was intended to hunt for targets on the surface of the sea rather than in the air, but with some reconfiguration, it could be made to work as an AEW radar.

The large scanner could not fit underneath the Sea King, so an installation was sketched out where it was placed on a rotating arm out

LEFT: The Searchwater radar installation of the Westland Sea King AEW7 ZE422, created in just a few weeks in 1982 to assist the task force recovering the Falklands from Argentine forces. The radome is inflatable.
Matthew Willis

the side of the fuselage, stowed beside the aircraft for take-off and landing, and swung down when in flight to provide a clear view beneath the helicopter.

The various problems to be addressed by the Project LAST (Low Altitude Surveillance Task) team included fitting the operating equipment inside the cabin, mitigating the inevitable vibration, and not least, availability of radar sets, which had been allocated to the RAF.

Westland Helicopters was fully behind the project, and the MOD quickly signed off the proposal. It was deemed feasible, and two Sea Kings were made available to modify, with a target of completing them within eight weeks.

The RAF refused the transfer of Searchwater sets that were awaiting installation in its Nimrod patrol aircraft, but an RAF officer at the MOD authorised the Royal Navy to

take two sets that were being used in a development programme. It was decided that HMS *Illustrious*, the second of the new Invincible-class carriers, would take the AEW Sea Kings to the South Atlantic when she departed on August 2, which meant the installation had to be finished and tested by then. Sea Kings XV650 and XV704 were ready in time and sailed for the Falklands less than three months after the project was first conceived.

As it turned out, hostilities ceased on June 20, but *Illustrious* remained on station until October 21, when land-based aircraft were stationed on the islands, to police the peace, and the presence of the two Sea Kings doubtless boosted confidence in the navy force. The conversion formed the basis of the Sea King AEW2 and AEW7, which went on to serve with the Fleet Air Arm for another 36 years.

BELOW: Westland Sea King AEW7 ZE 418 with the Searchwater radar in the deployed position.
Matthew Willis

NEW CARRIER NAVIES

In the jet age, a number of smaller navies challenged the status quo and broke into the world of carrier aviation.

BELOW: F2H Banshee #126337, '144' of the Royal Canadian Navy squadron VF-871 at Shearwater, Nova Scotia, where the aircraft were based when not embarked.
Library and Archives Canada Photo, MIKAN No. 4951172

On paper, the jet age should have put the aircraft carrier out of reach of smaller navies. In practice, carrier aviation blossomed as propellers gave way to jets. By the mid-1960s, there were five times as many navies operating aircraft carriers as at the end of World War Two!

Until well into World War Two, operating aircraft carriers was an expensive business. The ships themselves were large, complicated, and challenged the capacity of even the major naval nations, the US, UK, Japan, and France. The aircraft typically took longer to develop than land-based equivalents, and cost far more per airframe.

In the immediate aftermath of the war, the number of navies operating carriers had fallen to two – the British Royal Navy (RN) and the US Navy (USN).

There was, however, considerable enthusiasm for aircraft carriers among smaller navies. Personnel from Allied countries had experienced carrier operations first hand – the British Fleet Air Arm (FAA) formed squadrons from free Dutch and French personnel, and the FAA experienced an influx of volunteer reservists from across the Commonwealth.

As the jet age drew on, the cost and difficulty of developing a domestic capability in carrier aircraft and the ships to operate them did not diminish. It took until the 1960s for the French Marine Nationale to join the RN and USN, and until the 1970s for the Military Maritime Fleet of the USSR to bring the number of navies with organic carrier forces back up to four.

However, one major factor changed in the meantime. This was the availability of ships and aircraft off the shelf – and the willingness of major carrier navies to share them.

The huge expansion of the USN and RN carrier forces in the latter part of World War Two was partly achieved by the creation of so-called Light Fleet Carriers. These were vessels that were smaller, cheaper, and quicker to build than main fleet carriers but still capable enough to serve with the battle fleet, unlike escort carriers converted from merchant ships.

In 1942, the RN charged Vickers to come up with a design based on a simplified and slightly scaled down version of the contemporary Illustrious-class carrier, lacking armour, and powered by an adapted cruiser powerplant. Crucially, this would be capable of being produced quickly by commercial shipyards. Sixteen ships of the Colossus-class and the slightly improved Majestic-class were launched before the end of the war, ten being commissioned and four being in service by VJ-Day.

The USN meanwhile decided to use the hulls of light cruisers already under construction. The resulting Independence-class ships were smaller and less capable than the Colossus-class, but available sooner. Nine were completed, and eight survived the war, when they were quickly put into reserve.

This created a pool of little-used or brand new aircraft carriers which could operate modern aircraft. They could be operated by any mid-sized navy as easily as a cruiser, and the availability of trained, experienced aircrews and surplus aircraft made the idea highly attractive.

Finally, as the Cold War began, the major naval nations saw great value in building alliances with partner nations through organisations such as NATO by supplying smaller navies with equipment and training.

As the RN inevitably shrank in the years after the war, the Colossus-class carriers started to become surplus to requirements, while the incomplete Majestic-class ships were available immediately. The RN recognised the attractiveness of these carriers to allied navies, and offered them for sale, accelerating work on each of the Majestic-class ships as a buyer was found for it.

France purchased HMS *Colossus*, and the Independence-class ships *Belleau Wood* and *Langley*, while the Marine Nationale worked towards carriers of domestic design and construction. A number of other **»**

ABOVE: F2H Banshee #126295, '112' of the RCN squadron VF-870 banking over Dartmouth Naval Base, 1960–62, carrying a pair of AIM-9 Sidewinder missiles.
Author's collection

light fleet carriers, eight British and one American, would pass to navies which had never before operated their own carriers.

Canada

The Royal Canadian Navy grew from small beginnings to hold a significant role in the Battle of the Atlantic. In 1944, the RCN was given effective control of two RN escort carriers, providing the captain and the majority of the crew.

The RCN's major role of protecting sea lines of communication meant that carrier capability was felt to be vital. The Canadian government agreed to fund a light fleet carrier, and from 1946 to 1952, the RCN operated a loaned RN carrier with the option to buy.

By the 1950s, it was clear that jets were the future of carrier aviation, with modifications such as angled flight deck and steam catapults necessary. The RCN decided to buy one of the unfinished carriers, HMS *Powerful*, and have her completed with the most advanced features of carrier design that had emerged since the end of the war (see Rethinking the Carrier).

HMS *Powerful* was renamed HMCS *Bonaventure*. She was completed at Harland and Wolff's yard in Belfast with a sponson to port for the angled deck, and catapults and arrester gear capable of handling aircraft up to 24,000lb all-up weight. The lifts were also enlarged to suit larger aircraft.

Reflecting a shift in strategic focus from the UK to the US, the aircraft operated by this British-build carrier would all be American. Replacing the Hawker Sea Fury and Fairey Firefly fighters were 16 ex-USN McDonnell F2H-3 Banshee all-weather fighters, for which two squadrons were formed, 870 and 871. For anti-submarine warfare, *Bonaventure*

carried propeller powered Grumman Trackers and Sikorsky HO4S helicopters.

The shift to American aircraft made sense for the RCN, as squadrons could make use of US training facilities, and operate from USN carriers when *Bonaventure* was unavailable.

The RCN's Banshees began to arrive from 1955 and were mostly occupied in training and NATO exercises in the Atlantic for the next few years. The Sidewinder missile was added after trials in November 1959. *Bonaventure* shifted to anti-submarine warfare from 1960, with NATO focussing on the threat from Soviet ballistic missile submarines. The Banshees were increasingly subject to unserviceability, after years of operation in the tough Atlantic environment, and losses from accidents. As many as 12 of the 39 aircraft operated by the RCN – just over 30% – were written off between their introduction in November 1955 and retirement in September 1962. When the Banshees were withdrawn due to budget cuts, they were not replaced, and the RCN's Fleet Air Arm became a helicopter-only service.

Netherlands

The Koninklijke Marine (KM, the Royal Netherlands Navy) had, like the RCN, been keen to get into the carrier club from before the end of World War Two, to protect and police the country's overseas colonies.

They initially operated an escort carrier before replacing it with a Colossus-class which was renamed *Karel Doorman*. This was equipped with propeller types until the KM decided in 1955 it should be modernised to operate jets.

In 1958, *Karel Doorman* emerged from the dockyard with an angled

deck, steam catapult and up-to-date equipment including long-range radar of domestic design.

Unlike the RCN, the KM stuck with aircraft of British origin, buying Hawker Sea Hawk Mk 50 fighter-bombers to equip 3 and 860 Squadrons, although her anti-submarine aircraft were US-built propeller types. Like the RCN's Banshees, the KM Sea Hawks were upgraded to accept Sidewinder heat-seeking missiles in 1959.

Karel Doorman sailed to the East Indies in 1960 in response to the Western New Guinea crisis. The Dutch East Indies gained independence from the Netherlands in 1949, becoming Indonesia. The Netherlands prepared the Dutch-controlled part of New Guinea for independence, only for Indonesia to claim the territory and take steps to seize it, with the support of the USSR.

The carrier arrived on August 2, 1960, and her Sea Hawks overflew Hollandia, the capital of Dutch New Guinea to announce her arrival.

Indonesia responded to the carrier's arrival with a plan to sink her using Soviet-supplied Tu-16 bombers equipped with air-launched anti-ship missiles.

US diplomacy persuaded the Netherlands to hand over control of the colony to a UN administration, defusing the crisis.

With the independence of the former colonies, and the role of NATO navies changing from commerce protection to anti-submarine warfare, the KM retired its Sea Hawks in October 1964. *Karel Doorman* then only operated propeller types and helicopters. She was withdrawn following a fire in 1968, and although she was repaired and her machinery renewed, the Dutch government decided she was

BELOW: Hawker Sea Hawk FGA50 landing on HNLMS *Karel Doorman* in 1959. Netherlands Ministry of Defence

no longer needed and sold her to Argentina two years later.

Australia

Like the RCN, after World War Two the Royal Australian Navy was focussed on the protection of communication lines. The RAN acquired two as-yet incomplete Majestic-class light fleet carriers in 1947, concluding that carrier aviation would be central to its postwar purpose. The first was completed as designed, the second, HMAS *Melbourne*, was to be completed at a slower rate to enable modifications to operate larger and heavier aircraft, with jets already in mind. After construction recommenced in 1949, postwar innovations were included, and as such, when *Melbourne* commissioned in 1955, she was one of the first carriers to be completed with an angled deck.

Like *Bonaventure*, *Melbourne* operated jets from the start. Two fighter squadrons, 805 and 808, were equipped with de Havilland Sea Venom all-weather fighters, while two anti-submarine squadrons, 816 and 817, received Fairey Gannets. The Sea Venoms, with their air interception radar, were the first military jets in the region of Oceania that could operate at night.

Melbourne and her aircraft participated in a number of international naval exercises in Australasian and southeast Asian waters over the next few years, as well as flag-showing and training deployments. In March 1963, she recorded her 20,000th deck landing.

In 1959, the Australian government announced that the Sea Venoms and Gannets would not be replaced after they ran out of useful life, instead, the service switching entirely to helicopter-based anti-submarine warfare. However, this decision was reversed in 1963 due to the increasing instability in southeast Asia. The RAN decided to acquire new combat aircraft, and to extend the life of the current fixed wing air group until the new aircraft could arrive.

Australia, like Canada, had shifted its main strategic relationship from the UK to the US, and in 1965, ordered 10 A-4 Skyhawks and 14 Grumman S-2 Trackers, which were embarked in September 1967.

The appearance of the A-4 was something of a godsend for navies operating smaller carriers of late World War Two-vintage. The small and light jet went against the trend of ever larger and heavier carrier aircraft. It was able to operate from smaller flight decks and was still competitive in the mid-1960s. Continued upgrades would keep it so for many more years. The Australian Skyhawks would be tailored to RAN needs, with an air-defence capability as well as attack.

Brazil

The Marinha do Brasil (MdB, Brazilian Navy) became the first South American nation to purchase an aircraft carrier (though not the first to operate one) with the acquisition of a Colossus-class carrier from the UK in 1956. The reasons for this are disputed, and Brazil's then President Juscelino Kubitschek, who authorised its purchase, later claimed he had only done so to avoid a naval rebellion.

HMS *Vengeance* was renamed *Minas Gerais* and from 1957–60 was upgraded to modern standards in the Netherlands, where the experience of modernising *Karel Doorman* was fresh in the memory. The carrier arrived in Rio de Janeiro now capable of operating modern naval combat aircraft. Unfortunately, due to politics and a bitter rivalry between the MdB and the Força Aérea Brasileira (FAB, Brazilian Air Force), the navy was prevented from setting up a full naval air arm. *Minas Gerais* was restricted to helicopters and propeller-driven anti-submarine types until 1999, outside the scope of this publication, when A-4 Skyhawks were acquired.

Argentina

The Armada de la República Argentina (ARA, Argentine Navy) acquired HMCS *Warrior*, an unmodernised Colossus-class

»

BELOW: Hawker Sea Hawk FGA50s of 3 and 860 Squadrons parked on deck on HNLMS *Karel Doorman*, armed with practice rockets, while Grumman Avenger anti-submarine aircraft prepare to take off. Netherlands Ministry of Defence

LEFT: De Havilland Sea Venoms of the Royal Australian Navy's 808 Squadron on a training flight over England while working up in January 1956, still wearing Royal Navy markings but with the squadron flash on the tip tanks.
Author's collection

ship in 1958 and renamed her ARA *Independencia* – the first carrier operated in South America. Although the ARA's air arm received jet-powered Grumman F9F Panthers and Cougars from 1963 (see pages 28-29), these did not operate from *Independencia* as her catapults were inadequate. The carrier operated only propeller types apart from one trial landing with an F9F-2.

The Netherlands sold the modernised *Karel Doorman* to the ARA in 1970, as ARA *Veinticinco de Mayo*. Now the ARA had a carrier capable of operating its jets, though it is unclear if the F9Fs ever flew from her. In 1971 the ARA purchased 16 Douglas A-4s, which were embarked at New York the following year.

In 1978, the ARA agreed with France the purchase of 14 Dassault Super Étendard maritime strike aircraft and a supply of Aérospatiale Exocet anti-ship missiles to equip the 2nd Naval Air Attack Squadron. Five of these were to join *Veinticinco de Mayo*'s air group along with 10 Skyhawks and five S-2 Trackers. From 1980, a programme of upgrades was made to the carrier to support the French aircraft. Even though it was a small and light aircraft by contemporary standards, the Colossus-class ship still needed strengthening of the deck, and rearrangements to the hangar to fit all the aircraft in.

The ARA had five Super Étendards operational by the time of the

Falklands invasion in 1982, but the squadron had not completed carrier qualification. This restricted the type to land-based use for the duration of the conflict.

For the invasion of the Falklands, *Veinticinco de Mayo* joined Task Force 20, a covering force for the landings, with three A-4 Skyhawks embarked. She was at sea in late April for a planned attack on the

Royal Navy task force that had arrived to take back the islands, but unfavourable winds prevented the Skyhawks from launching. News that a Royal Navy submarine had sunk the cruiser ARA *Belgrano* caused the ARA to withdraw the carrier, and thereafter her aircraft only operated from land until Argentina's defeat .

A significant problem with the Colossus and Majestic-class ships

BELOW: Sea Venom of 805 Squadron, Royal Australian Navy, about to land on HMAS *Melbourne*.
Author's collection

ABOVE: A-4G Skyhawks 274 and 277 of 805 Squadron, Royal Australian Navy, parked on the stern of HMAS *Melbourne* at anchor in the 1970s. Author's collection

BELOW: A-4G Skyhawk 886 of 805 Squadron, Royal Australian Navy, in carrier landing configuration, carrying an ECM pod, in 1977. Two years later this aircraft washed off the deck of HMAS *Melbourne*. Author's collection

still in service was that their design speed of 25kts was problematic for launching high performance aircraft, and the remaining ships were by now rather well-used and heavy from repeated upgrades. In 1988, *Veinticinco de Mayo* could not exceed 18kts and was in poor condition, so was retired, ending the ARA's membership of the carrier club.

India

The Indian Navy established a modest naval air arm in 1955 but harboured much bigger ambitions. With India being responsible for the defence of a number of islands in the Indian Ocean, as well as for fleet defence, an aircraft carrier was deemed vital. Two years later, the unfinished Majestic-class ship HMS *Hercules* was purchased and taken in hand to be modified with the typical

upgrades required for operating jets. The ship was renamed *Vikrant* and commissioned in March 1961.

Her air group consisted of Sea Hawk FGA6 fighter-bombers, allocated to 300 Squadron 'White Tigers', and Breguet Alizé anti-submarine aircraft in 310 Squadron. A Sea Hawk was the first aircraft to perform a deck landing on May 18, 1961.

Vikrant was almost immediately dispatched to Goa while the Indian military annexed the Portuguese Indian territory to dissuade any outside intervention.

The confrontation with Pakistan in 1965 coincided with a refit so *Vikrant* took no part. The situation was almost repeated with the Indo-Pakistan War 1971, as the ship was awaiting replacement boilers, but such was the pressure to ensure her involvement that she was

brought out of dock to take part in operations despite not being able to exceed 14kts. The Sea Hawks of 300 Squadron distinguished themselves with low-level rocket and strafing attacks against Pakistan Navy gunboats and transport shipping in and around Pakistani ports.

The Sea Hawks served reliably and effectively into the early 1980s, despite being on paper completely outmoded, with supplementary aircraft bought from the German Navy. From the 1970s, however, the British Harrier VTOL jet was being aggressively marketed, and the Indian Navy acquired 30 of the naval Sea Harrier variant (see pages 74-75) as a replacement, the first »

ABOVE: An Indian Navy Sea Harrier FRS1 23 being serviced on the deck of INS *Viraat*.
NARA

operating fixed-wing aircraft, but the Harrier changed all that.

As part of Hawker Siddeley's energetic marketing, John Farley landed a Harrier aboard *Dédalo* in August 1972 off Barcelona. The demonstration was a game-changer, but for political reasons it was not possible to buy aircraft directly from the UK. British-built Harrier Mk55s designated 'AV-8S Matador' were acquired through the US Marine Corps in 1976. The carrier's wooden deck was skinned with metal to withstand the Harriers' jet blast, but otherwise the 30-year-old carrier was able to operate the jet in the air defence and attack role.

Spain sought to replace its AV-8S aircraft with second-generation Harriers in the 1980s and bought 12 AV-8B Matador II aircraft. A desire for greater air defence capability, with concurrent interest from Italy, led to British Aerospace and McDonnell Douglas developing the Harrier II Plus – a next generation Harrier with air-defence capability, including radar and increased missile compatibility. In 1990, Spain bought eight aircraft. By now *Dédalo* had been replaced by the new *Príncipe de Asturias*.

aircraft arriving in 1983. A few years later, the Indian Navy purchased HMS *Hermes*, which was adapted for Harrier operations, and renamed her *Viraat*.

The Sea Harriers served for 33 years, assisted with an upgrade to multi-mode radar allowing beyond-visual-range missiles to be used, though numbers fell to 11 by the type's retirement.

Spain
The availability of the VTOL Harrier in the 1970s had the effect of giving

small, World War Two-era light carriers a new lease of life. Hawker Siddeley offered the jet to numerous small navies including Argentina, but the first to seize the opportunity was the Armada Española, the Spanish Navy. The Armada developed carrier ambitions as early as the 1950s, hoping to buy an Essex-class carrier, but in 1967 settled on a more modest outcome of an Independence-class light carrier operating helicopters – USS *Cabot*, renamed *Dédalo*. At the time there was no question of

Italy
The Italian Marina Militare expressed interest in Harriers as early as the late 1960s, but rules preventing the navy from operating

RIGHT: An air-to-air view of AV-8S Matador 01-814 of the Spanish Navy above the Independence-class carrier *Dedalo* in the Mediterranean in 1988, taken by Lieutenant Commander John Leenhouts from an A-7E Corsair.
National Archives, NAID: 6430231

LEFT: AV-8B #164129, formerly of the US Marine Corps, serving as the prototype for the Harrier II Plus programme for the Italian and Spanish Navies in 1992. The new radar is apparent in the larger nose radome. Author's collection

fixed wing aircraft stymied plans until the late 1980s. In a competition between the British Sea Harrier FA2 and the American AV-8B, the Marina Militare chose the latter in May 1989. From 1991, the aircraft began to equip Gruppo Aerei Imbarcati, operating from the light carrier *Giuseppe Garibaldi*. The squadron took part in operations off the coast of Somalia in 1995, during the withdrawal of UN forces.

The MM found itself missing the air defence capability that had been offered by the Sea Harrier, and jointly with Spain and the US, commissioned the Harrier II Plus which offered radar and beyond-visual-range missiles, buying 12 of them in 1990.

Thailand

Thailand established a naval air arm as early as the 1950s. In the 1990s, the Royal Thai Navy eyed the possibilities offered by the Harrier. Perhaps surprisingly, they opted for a brand new ship, HTMS *Chakri Naruebet*, which was essentially a scaled-down *Príncipe de Asturias* but old aircraft, buying first-generation AV-8S Matadors from Spain as that country's navy had the much more capable EAV-8B. Seven Matadors were acquired in 1993 to equip 301 Squadron, with aircrews trained at Rota in 1995.

The Royal Thai Navy struggled to maintain good levels of serviceability, and it was reported that frequently only two of the aircraft were available. Deployments aboard *Chakri Naruebet* were relatively rare. The Matadors are believed to have been retired in 2006.

BELOW: The Royal Thai Navy carrier HTMS *Chakri Naruebet*, laid down in 1994, with an AV-8S Harrier on deck. NARA

DASSAULT SUPER ÉTENDARD

Conceived as a lightweight ground attack aircraft for the French Air Force, the Étendard IV M and Super Étendard became some of the most feared naval strike aircraft of the jet era.

RIGHT: Dassault Super Étendard of Flottille 11F 'Les Furieux', the first Aéronavale unit to operate the type, carrying an Exocet missile on the port wing and a 1,100l external tank on the starboard, in 1983. Matthew Willis

RIGHT: Dassault Étendard IV P, the specialist reconnaissance version, of Flottille 16F, in 1973. This unit operated the type from 1964 to 2000, seeing action in Bosnia in the 1990s. Note the camera bays in the nose and ventral pylon. Ray Thompson

BELOW: Super Étendard No 6 of Flottille 11F during a catapult launch from the carrier *Clemenceau* with a test version of the Exocet anti-ship missile in 1979–80. Author's collection

The Dassault Super Étendard became one of the most notorious naval aircraft of the jet age in the early 1980s. The subsonic light strike jet proved a highly effective platform for the Aérospatiale Exocet anti-ship missile, sinking several vessels during the Falklands conflict and the 'Tanker War' in the Persian Gulf.

The Étendard IVM and the developed Super Étendard began with a programme for a lightweight strike fighter for low-level operations for the Armée de l'Air (French Air Force) in the early 1950s.

Various versions of the new design were initially named Mystère XXII–XXVI, later renamed Étendard II–IV but retaining an obvious family resemblance to Dassault's Mystère series. The Étendard was designed for efficiency at high subsonic speeds, without the complexity of afterburning engines or the airframe strength necessary for supersonic flight. An important development was advanced high-lift devices to reduce landing-speed – a useful characteristic for operation from forward bases, but also essential for carrier operations, for which the type's small size and low weight was also attractive – Dassault began to consider possible naval versions in 1955.

In November 1954, the French Air Force ordered a prototype of the Étendard IV, the variant to be powered by a Snecma Atar 101 turbojet. At the same time, Dassault proposed a carrier-capable version with adaptations such as folding wings, arrester gear, and naval equipment.

The Armée de l'Air's test programme showed the Étendard IV to be a capable ground-attack aircraft and low-altitude fighter, which increased the interest of the Aéronavale, the French naval air arm. The Armée de l'Air lost interest in favour of developing the Mirage III, but the Aéronavale liked what they'd seen and ordered a navalised prototype as the Étendard IV M (for Marine). This flew in May 1958, and the following year 90 were ordered, 30 of them an unarmed photographic reconnaissance variant designated IV P.

Into Service

For carrier operation, the Étendard IV M/P featured large double-slotted trailing-edge flaps while the inner leading edge could droop to further increase lift. The type also had perforated spoilers on the upper surface of the wing for additional roll control. The wings folded outboard of the ailerons. The IV M was capable of air-to-air refuelling to increase range, which was only moderate on internal fuel. It was fitted with a very compact Aida radar and an infra-red sensor beneath the nose.

Production aircraft were delivered between December 1961 and May 1965, in time to equip the French Navy's two new aircraft carriers, *Clemenceau* and *Foch*. The first deployments took place in 1962.

The type was popular with pilots for its manoeuvrability, but by the end of the decade, the navy was considering a replacement. The preferred solution was a naval version of the Jaguar strike aircraft, but when carrier trials proved difficult and costs climbed, Dassault proposed an updated version of the Étendard.

The Super Étendard had aerodynamic improvements, a more powerful engine, greater fuel load, upgraded avionics, and a more capable radar, which resulted in a larger, slightly drooping nose. Three Étendard IV Ms were modified to

ÉTENDARD DATA

Étendard IV M

Length	14.35m (47ft 1in)
Span	9.60m (31ft 6in)
Height	3.85m (12ft 10in)
Empty weight	5,897kg (13,001lb)
Maximum weight	10,200kg (22,487lb)
Maximum speed	1,099 kph (683mph)
Range	3,300km (2,100 miles)
Engine	One × Snecma Atar 08B, 9,700lb thrust
Armament	Air-to-air missiles, Matra R550 Magic or AIM-9 Sidewinder, Air-surface missiles, Nord AS20 or AS30, guns, two × 30mm DEFA + 150 rounds per gun, two × Matra 68mm 18-rocket pods, bombs up to 3,000lb

Super Étendard

As Étendard IV M unless otherwise specified

Empty weight	6,450kg (14,220lb)
Maximum weight	11,900kg (26,235lb)
Maximum speed	1,099kph (683mph)
Range	1,820km (1,130 miles)
Engine	Snecma Atar 8K-50, 11,000lb thrust
Armament	Guns as IV M + 125 rounds per gun, air-to-surface missiles as IV M + Exocet anti-ship missile or ASMP nuclear stand-off weapon, Bombs up to 2,100lb including laser-guided, targeting and countermeasures pods.

ÉTENDARD TIMELINE

First flight (Étendard IV) – July 24, 1956

First flight (Étendard IV M) – May 21, 1958

Carrier trials – September 19, 1960

First production aircraft delivered – December 9, 1961

First squadron formed – April 18, 1962

Initial carrier deployment, *Clemenceau* –October 17, 1962

Super Étendard first flight – October 28, 1974

Carrier deployment Super Étendard – December 1978

Service entry Argentine Navy – November 1981

First combat – May 4, 1982 (Falklands)

Air strikes on Lebanon – September 22, 1983

Withdrawal IV M – July 1991

Operations over Bosnia begin – September 7, 1993

Last combat deployment (against IS) – December 2015–March 2016

Withdrawal from service – July 16, 2016

ABOVE: Super Étendard No59 of Flottille 11F in flight in 1988, carrying a 600l tank beneath each wing.
Marine Nationale

serve as prototypes, proving that the excellent handling characteristics remained, while the new wing with its 'dog tooth' leading edge allowed a greater weight of fuel and stores to be carried. The new electronic suite significantly increased the aircraft's capability, including operation of the Exocet anti-ship missile. However, range was reduced significantly

Aircraft began to arrive at frontline squadrons in 1978, the first being Flottille 11F, initially serving alongside the IV M/P. In addition to 71 Aéronavale Super Étendards, the Argentine Navy purchased 14, which it received in the second half of 1981.

The IV M remained in frontline use until 1991, while IV Ps were modernised, and were not retired until 2000.

The Super Étendard became the best known version, however, and the one with the most combat experience. In French service, Super Étendards supported French peacekeepers in Lebanon, NATO forces in Kosovo in 1999, and saw action in Afghanistan and Libya in the 2000s–2010s. Exocet-armed aircraft loaned to Iraq in 1983 sank several oil tankers in the 'Tanker War' dispute over shipping in the Persian Gulf.

Argentine Super Étendards saw the most dramatic combat use in the Falklands in 1982. Despite France suspending deliveries of aircraft and missiles during the conflict, Exocet-armed aircraft operating from land bases sank the Royal Navy destroyer HMS *Sheffield* and the transport *Atlantic Conveyer*.

Modernisation programmes from the late 1980s kept the aircraft in Aéronavale service until 2017, with additional capability including new radar, 'glass cockpit' and modern countermeasures. As of 2024, Argentina still operates the type.

BELOW: Modernised Super Étendard No46 of Flottille 11F in 2011, in landing condition with flaps, airbrakes, and hook extended. The retractable IFR probe is also extended.
Matthew Willis

THE FALKLANDS CONFLICT

The Falklands conflict of 1982 pitted the new and unproven UK light carriers, and their Vertical Take-Off and Landing jets, against seasoned French and American carrier types from the Argentine Navy.

It was a war that neither side expected to fight, and neither side was prepared for. When Argentina invaded the Falkland Islands, a British territory in the South Atlantic, on April 2, 1982, the militaries of both sides rushed to organise their forces as well as they could. Carrier aircraft and their crews were critical to both sides. On the Argentine side, the naval air forces were the reason the air attacks took such a toll on the British fleet. On the British side, quite simply, without the carriers and their aircraft, the war would have been lost before it started.

Argentina had been under the control of a string of military dictators since 1976. In 1981, amid economic and social collapse, a new junta took control, led by General Leopoldo Galtieri, Air Brigadier Basilio Lami Dozo, and Admiral Jorge Anaya.

Since the country was founded in the early 1800s, Argentina had intermittently pressed a claim to the Falkland Islands, which lay 400 miles off the South American coast. The islands had been governed by the UK since 1833, though had earlier been occupied by settlements of various nationalities. The sovereignty of the islands was a touchstone for Argentine nationalists, and Admiral Anaya proposed to bolster the government's crumbling popularity by seizing them. He assured Galtieri and Lami Dozo that the British would be reluctant to respond militarily and could not if they wanted to due to the rundown of British military forces, particularly in relation to the ability to project power globally. HMS *Ark Royal*, the last conventional carrier, was being broken up. Even though three new light 'Harrier Carriers' had been ordered, two were not yet finished and the first, HMS *Invincible,* was to be sold to Australia less than a year after becoming operational.

The invasion was originally proposed for 1983, the 150th anniversary of the British establishing control over the islands, though it was moved forward to April 1982. Plans for the operation, codenamed Rosario, were finalised on March 22, 1982.

Rosario was based around two task groups of the Armada de la República Argentina (ARA), the Argentine Navy. The first, Task Group 40, was responsible for inserting Marines ashore. Task Group 20 was responsible for reconnaissance offshore and covering the landings against any opposition from the sea. This group included the aircraft carrier *Veinticino de Mayo* which from March 28, flew combat air patrols (CAP) with A-4Q Skyhawks of the 3a Escuadrilla.

On April 1, the Argentine Marines went ashore. The presence of *Veinticino de Mayo* offshore was reported by British Royal Marines at Camber Peninsula, indicating that

BELOW: The Argentine aircraft carrier *Veinticino de Mayo* in port during Exercise Unitas XX, on June 1, 1979. Her sole contribution to the war was to cover the invasion force. For reasons that aren't clear, she failed to launch her aircraft in a strike on May 2, and retreated to port thereafter. US National Archives, ID 6351906

the situation was serious. After a brief but bloody fight with the heavily outnumbered resident Royal Marine detachment, the Argentine flag was hoisted over the Falklands.

'The Empire Strikes Back'

Contrary to Admiral Anaya's insistences, the British government was determined to respond militarily, and the military – particularly the Royal Navy – insisted it was possible to take the islands back. Central to these plans were HMS *Invincible* and HMS *Hermes*, an older light carrier that

had been converted to operate the British Aerospace (formerly Hawker Siddeley) Sea Harrier until the second and third Invincible-class carriers came on stream.

Air power – and particularly naval air power – would be critical to both sides, though this was less obvious on the Argentine side. For the British, RAF combat aircraft were mostly far out of range. Only a few long range bombers could reach the islands, and only then with an immense in-flight refuelling operation. Air superiority was critical for British forces to carry out

the planned amphibious landings. It could only come from carrier-based aircraft.

The trouble for the Royal Navy was that even with two carriers on the scene, they would only have a handful of fighters.

Overall, during the conflict, 171 naval aircraft from 15 Naval Air Squadrons were deployed. However, the vast majority of these were helicopters. The two operational Sea Harrier squadrons, 800 and 801, mustered a mere ten aircraft between them. This was doubled with transfers of aircraft from ➤➤

the HQ unit, 899 Squadron, testing establishments and storage.

The scramble for pilots was just as frantic, with personnel recalled from exchanges with the US Marine Corps and RAF, and others borrowed from the RAF.

The loss rate in the Sea Harrier force would likely be high. While the existing squadrons prepared to head south, a third squadron, 809 was hurriedly formed to provide reinforcements during the battle for

the islands, and it would provide a further eight aircraft and crews for them, which in practice were shared between 800 and 801 Squadrons. This brought the total to 28. Would it be enough?

With virtually every Sea Harrier yet built on its way south, the RAF agreed to provide the carriers' air groups with six Harrier GR3s and crews for them. Aircraft and pilots from 1(F) Squadron were chosen, because they had recently trained

in air combat, and if they were needed to replace lost Sea Harrier pilots, they would need to be able to fight Argentine aircraft. The GR3, however, had no radar or targeting system. Air combat would have to be World War Two-style, using guns and the 'Mark One Eyeball.' The ability to fire Sidewinder missiles was being added, but target acquisition still had to be visual.

The 809 and 1(F) Squadron crews prepared themselves and their

aircraft as best they could in the UK as the carrier task group headed south, to join British forces in May.

The British carrier task force set out on April 5. It hoped to reach its objective in secret, but to the Royal Navy's surprise, the Argentineans used British communication satellite signals to help locate the fleet in transit with Boeing 707 airliners. The first time opposing aircraft made contact was on April 21 when a 707 appeared over the task force and was intercepted and shepherded away by Sea Harriers. The repurposed airliner continued to track the fleet until the British let it be known through diplomatic channels that if this continued, it would be shot down.

Battle joined

When the Fuerza Aérea Argentina, the Argentine Air Force (AAF), and the ARA's air arm learned of the invasion plans, it came as a shock. The AAF had not trained or developed tactics for maritime operations and had little idea how to counter the RN carrier task group.

The only force in the Argentine military with the training to attack ships was the ARA's air arm. This was, relatively speaking, a tiny force, with only 20 Skyhawks, five Super Étendards and a handful of pilots. The ARA quickly launched a training programme for AAF pilots to teach them the appropriate tactics and break the habits of their established practices. For example, AAF pilots were trained to enter a steep climb after releasing a bomb to avoid the risk of blast damage. Doing so on an anti-ship strike would make them a sitting duck for the fleet's AA defences. The pilots were also unused to just how low they would have to fly to get in and out safely – ideally no higher than 10ft above the wavetops! ARA pilot Lieutenant Benito Rotolo ruefully remarked that: "Sometimes air force pilots felt like they were low enough,

but they really weren't because they didn't survive."

Like the Sea Harriers and Harrier GR3s, the Super Étendards and their Exocet missiles were far from mission ready on the outbreak of war. The 2a Escuadrilla Aeronavale de Caza y Ataque had only formed four months beforehand and had only received five aircraft and the same number of Exocets. No more would be forthcoming for the foreseeable future, as a European Union arms embargo prevented any further aircraft or spares from being sent. The pilots had only basic training on the type which chiefly covered flying the aeroplane, not combat.

In fact, the aircraft and missiles had not yet been properly configured, and the British doubted the Exocets could be made operational without French support. When the Armada mechanics achieved this, it gave rise to suspicions that Aérospatiale technicians had assisted the Argentineans in contravention of the embargo, which France hotly denied. Either way, the Exocets could be used against British shipping, and only time would tell if it would be effective.

The task group arrived off the Falklands on May 1. The Argentine command assumed that the British would immediately launch an amphibious assault and conducted a 'maximum effort' attack with 56 aircraft, including 16 A-4 Skyhawks, 12 IAI Daggers, 10 Mirage IIIEAs and six Canberra bombers.

Of the 56 aircraft, only three Daggers located the British warships, bombing HMS *Glamorgan* and HMS *Alacrity*, but not scoring any hits. Meanwhile, Sea Harriers had intercepted several small groups of Argentine jets. In two engagements, each side tried to to manoeuvre into an attack position until the Argentine jets ran low on fuel and withdrew. In another engagement, two Mirages were shot down by Sidewinders after trying to dogfight with the Sea Harriers. A fourth encounter saw two Daggers intercepted – one launched a missile but was shot down by a Harrier. The fifth interception of the day came when the British CAP found one of two groups of Argentine Canberra bombers searching for targets. The Sea Harriers shot down one of the bombers and the rest turned tail. »

ABOVE: Westland Lynx HAS2 XZ230 of 815 Squadron at the International Air Tattoo 1981, carrying two Sea Skua missiles on the port weapons pylons – the squadron had several successes with this missile in the Falklands, and later during the Gulf War of 1991.
Ray Thompson

BELOW: Armada de la República Argentina (ARA) Douglas A-4Q Skyhawk #144882, a former US Navy aircraft upgraded and sold to Argentina in January 1972. This aircraft was embarked on *Veinticino de Mayo* from April 28 to May 10, then flew from Río Grande Naval Air Base. It flew in an attack on HMS *Antelope* on May 23.
Wikimedia Commons/ Chuckborri

It had been a costly first day for the AAF, losing four aircraft and causing no damage to the carrier task force.

The following day, May 2, came close to seeing the first carrier-to-carrier battle since World War Two. The *Veinticino de Mayo* was still at sea and the ARA hoped to locate the task group and capture it in a pincer, with the carrier's aircraft on one side and the cruiser ARA *General Belgrano*, armed with anti-ship missiles, on the other.

The carrier was prepared and eight Skyhawks ranged for launching at dawn. However, for reasons that have never been adequately explained, *Veinticino de Mayo*'s aircraft never took off. The weather, lack of reconnaissance information, and concerns over the A-4's range have been variously cited, but none seem convincing. Events later that day sealed the carrier's fate for the

rest of the battle. The *Belgrano* was sunk by a Royal Navy submarine, and the ARA withdrew all its major warships to port.

The ARA Skyhawks withdrew and threw themselves into training for the next anticipated major effort.

The losses on May 1, and the lack of amphibious landings, caused the Argentine command to dramatically reduce the number of air attacks until the expected assault took place.

Vertical Limit

The FAA Sea Harrier crews had unshakeable faith in their aircraft. In the few years they had been operating them, they had concluded that the SHAR, as it was affectionately known, was not just capable of warding off lumbering Soviet *Bears* and *Badgers* – it could dogfight modern combat jets and, in certain circumstances, come out best.

The first day's engagements only boosted their confidence.

It should not have been possible. The Harrier was designed as a low-level ground attack aircraft, and such machines typically have poor manoeuvrability in air combat. The Harrier's small wing gave it a fast low-level 'dash' but a poor turning rate at high speed. The ace up its sleeve was the swivelling nozzles that enabled hovering. Pilots discovered that manipulating the nozzles in flight gave the Harrier exceptional manoeuvrability at lower speed, and practice dogfights against various state-of-the-art fighters from other services proved that the Sea Harrier could hold its own.

However, it was an unescapable fact that the aircraft was still in an embryonic state. Its systems were nowhere near maturity, and nobody could be entirely sure that in the

An immature radar was better than no radar at all, but the timing left the Blue Fox as a flawed and variable benefit.

The RAF Harrier GR3s may have been in service longer, and consequently had more chances to work out the bugs, but when it came to operating from carriers they faced just as many challenges as the Sea Harriers.

It had long been anticipated that the RAF's Harriers would operate from the RN's carriers when the need arose. The trouble was that few aircraft had received the necessary modifications to enable the GR3s to operate safely and effectively from carriers. These included transponders for the pilot to locate the ship in instrument flying conditions, additional tie-down points, and anti-corrosion treatment. Steps were taken to make the modifications before the aircraft had to head to the warzone, but it was touch and go.

The most serious impediment to the GR3s operating from carriers was the aircraft's inertial navigation and attack system (INAS). This was a very sophisticated system developed for the stillborn TSR2, but it had to have its position fixed before every flight and needed to be stationary to do so. This was a serious drawback for an aircraft expected to operate from a ship. The FINRAE (Ferranti Inertial Rapid Alignment Equipment), a mobile trolley that could calibrate the INAS on deck, was developed to address this but in the spring of 1982, it was not working reliably, and the GR3 INAS would often lose its

position shortly after take-off. The pilots then had to resort to notepad and stopwatch to navigate.

The 1(F) pilots had a valuable opportunity on April 23 to train against French Mirage IIIs and Super Étendards of the type that they would face in the Falklands. This helped inform tactics. A Mirage would lose to a Harrier in a slow-speed turning fight. If the Mirage attempted to make slashing attacks, the Harrier's best defence would be to fly at low level to confuse the fighter's systems.

When 809 and 1(F) Squadrons were as ready as they could be, they flew to Ascension Island which was acting as a staging post for the operation, refuelling from RAF tankers as they went. The aircraft were loaded onto the container ship *Atlantic Conveyer*, which had a smaller 'Harrier deck' welded to it to enable the aircraft to fly directly onto the carriers when they arrived.

Exocet

Despite the decision to scale back air operations after the first bruising on May 1, the ARA did not keep its powder entirely dry. The Super Étendards of 2a Escuadrilla had transferred to Río Grande Naval Air Base in Patagonia, the closest base to the Falklands at some 450 miles. On May 4, two Super Étendards flew towards the islands at low level, 'popped up' to allow the radar to scan for targets and picked up a British warship. They launched their missiles – two of the five available – and made their escape. »

BELOW: Three Sea Harrier FRS1s from the first three frontline squadrons, from the nearest, 800, 801 and 899 Squadrons. The aircraft are wearing the all-over Extra Dark Sea Grey scheme with toned-down markings adopted for the Falklands. The nearest aircraft, XZ500, in the hands of Flight Lieutenant Leeming shot down an Armada Skyhawk on May 21, 1982. Author's collection

heat of combat, everything would work as it should. The Blue Fox radar was a marvel of packaging and later became an effective piece of equipment, but in April 1982 it was very much a work in progress. The development programme was abruptly stopped when news of the invasion reached the RN, to concentrate efforts on production. This left the radars in 800 and 801 Squadron's Sea Harriers at several different states of modification, and the pilots and technicians had varying experience in how to make them work. Some pilots got good results from the set – notably 801 Squadron under Lieutenant Commander Nigel 'Sharkey' Ward were more confident in it – but others found it unable to detect targets more than ten miles away, and aircraft at low level not at all.

The Exocets descended to just above sea level, following the track given to them by the Super Étendards' radar. When it was near the point indicated, it switched on its own radar, which immediately picked up a target, and it began to home in, and after a few moments slammed into the destroyer HMS *Sheffield*. The warhead failed to go off, but the ballistic effects of the impact were severe. Uncontrollable fires broke out, and eventually *Sheffield* was abandoned.

Meanwhile, the AAF had sent aircraft to the Falklands in 'penny packets,' aiming to erode the task group's strength while maintaining its own. In this, they were partially successful. HMS *Glasgow* was hit by a bomb from an FAA Skyhawk on May 12, but numerous aircraft were shot down by Sea Harriers, missiles, and guns.

Meanwhile, the Sea Harriers took part in ground attack sorties against Argentine positions ashore.

The additional eight Sea Harrier FRS1s from 809 Squadron and six RAF Harrier GR3s from 1(F) Squadron arrived with *Atlantic Conveyer* on May 20, and transferred to the carriers. It was not a moment too soon, as the amphibious landings were to take place at San Carlos Water from the following day. The Sea Harriers were shared between HMS *Invincible* and *Hermes*, while the RAF Harriers all went to the latter. As losses had not been as serious as feared, the GR3s were put to work at the job they knew best, low-level ground attack, tactical reconnaissance, and close support of troops. In this they had a considerable impact, despite the dangers posed by shoulder-launched anti-aircraft missiles and small-arms fire.

On May 21, D-Day for the amphibious landings, the Argentine command once again unleashed an all-effort onslaught against the fleet, with 75 sorties timed to arrive close together. Argentine naval

and air force fighter-bombers were able to penetrate British defences repeatedly, leading to the landing zone at San Carlos Water being nicknamed 'Bomb Alley'. The brunt of the attacks was borne by the escorting warships and not the troopships and amphibious warfare vessels, but the Argentine fighter bombers, generally operating without escort, did considerable damage. Ten warships, auxiliaries and supply ships were hit by air attacks between May 21 and 25, some of them severely. Three warships, an auxiliary and a supply ship were lost, the latter was the *Atlantic Conveyor*. The 2a Escuadrilla Super Étendards launched on May 25, hoping to find the carriers. Instead, their Exocets locked onto the container ship, causing fatal damage.

By early June, the air strikes had ebbed again, due

LEFT: Sea Harrier FRS1 XZ452 of 899 Squadron at RNAS Yeovilton a month before the Falklands War. XZ452 transferred to 801 Squadron and shot down a Mirage IIIEA while flown by Flight Lieutenant Barton on May 1, 1982, but was tragically lost along with Lieutenant Commander E.J. Eyton-Jones in an accident with XZ453 while on Combat Air Patrol east of the Falklands five days later. Ray Thompson

to poor weather, ever increasing AA defences, and the depredations of the Sea Harriers.

In the meantime, four further RAF Harriers managed to fly directly from Ascension using in-flight refuelling. It was a mammoth flight for a single-seat aircraft, but two managed it on June 1, and a further two on June 8. This brought the total number of Harriers in operation in the Falklands during the campaign to 38, though a number of Harriers of both types had been lost in the intervening period. The same day that the last Harriers arrived, a frigate and an RFA were bombed and severely damaged, showing that the Argentine air forces had not lost their teeth.

Counting the Cost

Argentine forces surrendered on June 14. All told, Argentine forces lost 102 aircraft, and 65 personnel from all air arms. British forces lost 35 aircraft, including six Sea Harriers and four Harrier GR3s, and 17 FAA personnel lost their lives.

Both sides were operating under numerous disadvantages.

The non-participation of *Veinticino de Mayo* meant that Argentine aircraft were all operating from land bases at a range of between 450 and 600 miles. The RN aircraft, however, were also operating at long distance due to the carriers being held out of Exocet range. This severely limited their time over the islands, but as the loss of one of the carriers would likely have ended the Task Force's chances of victory at a stroke, it was a necessary step.

Both forces lacked good reconnaissance – Argentine forces struggled to find the task group and never managed to find the carriers in strength, while British lack of airborne early warning left outlying ships highly vulnerable.

The Fleet Air Arm's Sea Harriers proved more effective than the Royal Navy's wildest hopes despite limited numbers of the aircraft, carrying out over 1,400 air defence and ground attack sorties. The Sea Harriers

destroyed 23 Argentine aircraft and proved more than a match for their opposition. The RAF Harriers, despite considerable technical challenges, made a very significant contribution, proving pivotal in the Battle of Goose Green, and proved to both RN and RAF bigwigs that RAF VTOL jets operating from carriers could be done effectively.

At times, though, Argentine air attacks stretched the British fleet's air defences to breaking point, finding, and probing the weaknesses in much-vaunted anti-aircraft missile systems, particularly the newer Sea Dart and Sea Wolf.

The ARA made good use of a small number of Exocet anti-ship missiles, with effective co-operation between strike and reconnaissance aircraft.

Ultimately, Argentinian air forces were, despite fierce resistance, unable to prevent the British amphibious assault from succeeding. While bombing and missile attacks caused significant setbacks for the British, air defence and air support ultimately made the recapture of the islands possible.

BELOW: HMS *Illustrious* returning to her home port of Portsmouth at the end of a commission. *Illustrious* was the second Invincible-class carrier to commission, completed quickly in September 1982 to sail to the Falklands and relieve HMS *Invincible*. Matthew Willis

McDONNELL DOUGLAS-BAE T-45 GOSHAWK

The T-45 Goshawk, result of a collaboration between British Aerospace and McDonnell Douglas, brought carrier jet training into the modern age. A heavily redesigned, carrier-capable version of the popular Hawk trainer, the Goshawk would train several generations of US Navy fast jet pilots.

RIGHT: T-45C #165485 '100', the personal aircraft of VT-7's commanding officer, Captain J.R. 'Woody' Wood, for the occasion of a Navy vs Army football game when it had its fuselage markings modified to read 'GO NAVY,' with 'BEAT ARMY' on the underside.
Matthew Willis

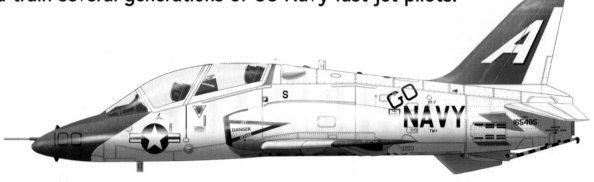

The US Navy (USN) began to look at a replacement for its existing intermediate and advanced trainers as early as 1973, but the programme was not finally authorised until 1979. The VTX-TS programme was of huge interest to the aircraft industry, both in the US and overseas, and the flurry of submissions included 14 manufacturers, several acting in partnership, and many of whom offered more than one entry.

The USN needed a trainer that would prepare pilots for the increasingly high-performance, high-tech fast jets that were recently in service or on the horizon.

Among the competitors was a partnership between British Aerospace (BAe) and McDonnell Douglas. These two companies had a strong existing working relationship through their partnership on F-4 Phantoms tailored to Royal Navy needs, and on the Harrier 'jump jet' where aircraft for the US Marine Corps were supplied under a licence agreement by McDonnell Douglas.

In January 1980, the two companies formalised the partnership, forming a joint team for the bid.

They offered two different types. An all-new type, and an adaptation of the proven BAe Hawk trainer which had been in service with the RAF since 1976 and was attracting a great deal of interest from air arms around the world. Thus far, however, it had been strictly land-based.

The 'Hawk VTX' as it was then termed, would need significant changes for the USN role. These included:

- Strengthening the airframe to take the loads of catapult launches and arrested landings
- Redesigning the landing gear for carrier operation, stronger and with longer travel than the standard Hawk undercarriage – the nose gear was all-new, with integral catapult tow-bar
- A tailhook was added under the rear fuselage
- The Hawk's single air brake, mounted beneath the fuselage, was replaced with two large air brakes on the fuselage sides
- The cockpit was redesigned with controls and displays more closely related to the new generation of combat aircraft.

BAe found that its chief competitor was the Hawk's old rival, the Dassault-Dornier Alphajet, in a joint entry between the European consortium and Lockheed.

In November 1981, the USN chose the Hawk VTX, to enter service under the designation T-45 Goshawk.

Taming the Goshawk
The development programme was arduous and introduced numerous further changes to the basic Hawk. The first development aircraft, #162787, was rolled out on March 16, 1988, and flew exactly a month later. A second aircraft, #162788, joined

RIGHT: Publicity artwork produced by the McDonnell Douglas-BAe team for the Hawk VTX programme in 1980. Author's collection

the programme in November that year. Flying took place at the Marine Corps Air Station at Yuma and the Navy Air Station at Patuxent River.

Low-speed handling was a particular priority, as for all carrier aircraft. The fin was increased in height, and leading edge slats were added to help maintain airflow over the wing surface at high angles of attack.

A particularly neat and innovative device made its appearance here. It became clear that the all-flying tailplane suffered interference from the air brakes in their new position on the fuselage sides, and this affected control on approach to land. The device was named the Side-Mounted Unit Root Fin, or 'SMURF'.

The design team considered ways to encourage smooth airflow to the tailplane when it was in its extreme 'nose down' position. A wing could be fitted with a leading edge root extension (LERX), but this would not work on a tailplane. The brainwave that restored clean airflow was like a LERX but fixed to the fuselage. In normal flight it was simply a fin attached to the fuselage that had no effect on flying characteristics. When the aircraft was landing, though, the tailplane's angle brought the leading edge in line with the fin, enabling it to direct clean airflow onto the tail.

The first production T-45A flew in late 1991 and was received by the navy in January 1992. For the next two years, instructors and training squadrons familiarised themselves with the new aircraft, as well as the training syllabus and simulators that were part of the package. Training on the T-45A began in 1994.

The Goshawk was clearly far more suitable for training pilots for the new, complex jets such as the F-14 Tomcat and F/A-18 Hornet than what had gone before. It was also

RIGHT: The first T-45, #162787, about to catch a hook on USS *John F Kennedy* in December 1991 during carrier trials, when the Goshawk made its first carrier landings...
Author's collection

BELOW: ...And catapult take-offs. The T-45 passed its trials and entered USN service the following month, January 1992.
Author's collection

T-45 GOSHAWK DATA

Length	11.97m (39ft 3in)
Span	9.39m (30ft 10in)
Height	4.27m (14ft 0in)
Empty weight	4,263kg (9,339lb)
Maximum weight	5,783kg (12,750lb)
Maximum speed	625mph
Range (internal fuel)	1,854km (1,152 miles)
Engine	One × Rolls-Royce Turbomeca Adour F405-RR-401, 5,845lb thrust
Armament	Three × weapon stations for practice bombs, two × rocket pods.

T-45 TIMELINE

Wins VTXTS competition – November 19, 1981

First flight – April 16, 1988

First carrier landing, USS *John F Kennedy* – December 4, 1991

Production aircraft flies – December 16, 1991

US Navy receives its first T-45A – January 23, 1992

First T-45 flight with a student pilot – February 11, 1992

Graduation of first class of pilots to qualify on T-45 – October 5, 1994

T-45C introduced into USN service – December 15, 1997

far more efficient – on average T-45 pilots qualified with a 25% reduction in flying hours compared with their predecessors on older types. The USN was able to maintain its training rates with fewer aircraft and personnel. Each T-45 typically flew more than 60 hours per month, demonstrating enviable levels of reliability.

Further developments kept it in line with ever developing technology, and from the 73rd production aircraft, a full 'glass cockpit' was added, with dials replaced by multi-function displays. Aircraft to this specification were designated T-45C, and eventually all Goshawks were upgraded to this standard.

Goshawks were based at the USN stations at Meridian, Mississippi, and Kingsville, Texas. Some 234 production aircraft were built, and the type remains in service as of 2024, 30 years after training their first students, though the USN has started looking for a replacement.

CARRIER JET TRAINERS

Training for carrier jet pilots is littered with difficulties. The jet era posed the conundrum of whether to introduce dedicated carrier training aircraft at great expense or find more creative solutions.

ABOVE: Prototype de Havilland Sea Vampire trainer WW458, trialled by the Fleet Air Arm in 1952, leading to an order for 73 land-based DH Sea Vampire T.22s. Ironically, when WW458 was withdrawn from flying in 1954 it went to the carrier HMS *Albion* to train the crew in handling aircraft on deck.
Author's collection

It is difficult to imagine landing a jet on an aircraft carrier without experiencing it. In 1990, US Navy Lieutenant M.C. Biemiller wrote of his first 'trap' in a T-45 Goshawk: "Before I knew what hit me, I had come to a complete stop in 1.2 seconds. It felt like hitting a brick wall at 125 miles per hour. It was 1,000 times more violent than I ever expected. You hear a bang as you hit the deck followed by a howling screech as the tail-hook grabs the arresting wire and the wire spools out. Inside the cockpit, every part of your body is thrown against the straps. Your legs and arms feel like they're just going to separate from your body."

Not for nothing is the art of carrier landing often referred to as a 'controlled crash.'

Carrier navies at the dawn of the jet age faced a dilemma. Jets handled differently to propeller aircraft both on the deck and in the air. Existing trainers would not fully prepare trainee pilots for service aircraft, and in the worst case could train the wrong reflexes in extremis. A dedicated carrier-capable jet trainer would address that but would use up scarce funds that would

otherwise be available for combat aircraft. Most of a trainee carrier pilot's flying took place from land anyway, and the deck landing part of basic training was relatively brief – there would be far more of it when a pilot got to advanced training and onto frontline types. With a deck-landing type, the number of aircraft purchased would be small, making them expensive per airframe, with shorter lives and a higher loss rate than land-based types. But would the savings outweigh the cost of naval pilots being less prepared for the high-stress, high-stakes business of deck landing?

LEFT: The North American Buckeye, in the early single-engined T-2A variant, with the training squadron VT-7 at Kingsville, Texas. VT-7 undertook jet transition, training in aerobatics, instruments, formation flying and gunnery, and finally carrier qualification.
Author's collection

Compromise approach

The Royal Navy's Fleet Air Arm decided not to introduce a dedicated, carrier capable jet trainer. Instead, it replaced its hooked Firefly and Sea Fury trainers with a version of the RAF's de Havilland Vampire trainer. The confusingly named Sea Vampire T.22 was strictly land-based, and only differed from the RAF T.11 in minor ways, such as radio fit. It was, nevertheless, extremely useful.

The Sea Vampire helped adapt existing pilots to the differences between propeller aircraft and jets. Some, such as operating the two kinds of engine, were obvious. Throttle response, torque (or lack thereof), and fuel consumption were all factors a new pilot had to get used to. Other differences were less obvious. Former Royal Australian Navy (RAN) pilot Norman Lee wrote: "Most of us found that the short, rounded nose of the Vampire made it difficult to establish an attitude visually after Sea Furies and Fireflys. We soon learnt that we had to use our instruments even in visual flight to fly the aircraft accurately; seat of the pants was on the way out. Also, because we were now flying at 30,000 feet plus, generally above cloud, instrument flying assumed much greater importance than it had in the past."

Even without the ability to make arrested landings and accelerated take-offs, the Sea Vampire could teach a certain amount about deck landing. The FAA and RAN used Sea Vampires to perform touch-and-go landings, which at least covered the approach part of the landing sequence.

However, some naval aviators considered it insufficient for a pilot to only have touch-and-goes under their belt before they deck-landed for real.

USN pilot Commander Graham C. Scarbro wrote in the US Naval Institute magazine *Proceedings*: "Assuming that a touch and go is the same as a trap and a cat is a decision that can only be reasonable to someone who has done neither. In all of naval history, there never has been a ramp strike (when a jet crashes into the back of the ship) on a planned touch and go. There have, however, been countless ramp strikes when pilots are trying to land aboard the ship with their tailhook down. When the pressure rises and getting aboard is a matter of life and death, landing aboard the ship becomes an intense physiological experience."

At least when the Royal Navy moved from conventional carriers to VTOL ships, it became easier. When the Sea Harrier FRS1 began to arrive in 1979, the FAA acquired three Mk T.4N two-seat Harriers with full dual controls, as the differences from the land-based two seater were relatively slight.

Adapted and new types

The French Aéronavale decided that it needed a basic trainer that was capable of arrested deck landings. The Fouga CM.175 Zéphyr was an adaptation of the Magister, modified with a tail hook, strengthened and corrosion-proofed airframe, beefed-up undercarriage, and myriad other small changes. Thirty were built though only 14 were used at any one time to stretch out airframe life. The Zéphyr served from the late 1950s to the mid-1990s, though by their retirement, the type bore little relation to the frontline types the Aéronavale operated.

Indeed, the Aéronavale soon felt the need to supplement the Zéphyr with a strictly land-based type that could do many of the things that the carrier capable type could do, such as navigation, weapons, and basic flight training, without using up valuable Zéphyr hours. In 1959, the service purchased 14 Morane-Saulnier MS.760 Paris aircraft, a four-seat twin-jet useable as a liaison type as well as a trainer. It was capable of weapons training and with tip tanks carried nearly twice the fuel load of the Zéphyr. Its side-by-side seating was also preferable to the Fouga's tandem seating. »

BELOW: A Morane-Saulnier MS.760 Paris, which the Aéronavale acquired to supplement its deck-landing trainers, seen in 1974. Ray Thompson

The US Navy adapted existing types as advanced trainers. Nearly 400 two-seat versions of the F9F Cougar, the F9F-8T, were acquired from 1956, and the trainer version of the A-4 Skyhawk, as the TA-4, followed from 1965.

The USN initially took the adaptation approach for its basic jet trainer too, with the Lockheed T2V Sea Star, a fully navalised version of the T-33 Shooting Star. The problems of adapting an existing type were stark when considering the Sea Star, which ended up a substantially different aeroplane: new undercarriage, high-lift devices, tail fin, and a reprofiled cockpit to give a better view for deck landing. It first flew in 1953 and did not enter full service until late 1957. A year before that, the USN issued a requirement for a carrier-capable trainer resulting in an entirely new type, the TJ2 (later T-2) Buckeye, which ended up replacing the Sea Star.

The USN put its requirements to the industry for a new carrier trainer in 1956. North American Aviation (NAA) won with a J-34-powered design; its straight wing derived from the FJ Fury fighter. The Buckeye went from specification to service in less time than the Sea Star took between its first flight and service entry, despite being based on an existing type. It entered service in 1959 and immediately proved its worth despite being underpowered. The single J34 engine of the early service T-2 was replaced in the early 1960s with two Pratt &

Whitney J60 jets, giving the T-2 its characteristic tubby appearance.

Its fundamentally good characteristics kept it in service until its resemblance to service aircraft wore paper thin, with its analogue cockpit and 1950s-era hardware.

Full-system approach

To replace both the Buckeye and the TA-4 in the late 1970s, the USN instigated a revolutionary approach. Rather than just buying an aeroplane, they wanted a full training system. The VTX-TS programme included aircraft, simulators, a complete training syllabus with all materials provided, and technical support for the life of the aircraft.

The requirement stimulated the industry to a remarkable degree, with multiple entries from numerous manufacturers, some of whom had no background in military aircraft. An airline was even involved in one bid. Designs ranged from an upgraded Buckeye to all-new aircraft, via navalised versions of existing trainers. The competition was won by the McDonnell Douglas-British Aerospace-Sperry bid with the 'Hawk VTX', which became the T-45 Goshawk (pages 110-111), finally combining the intermediate and advanced carrier training function in a single type which entered service in the early 1990s.